MARTIN CONWAY

The Undivided Vision

Students explore a worldly Christianity

> No man can look with undivided
> vision at God and the world of reality
> so long as God and the world are torn
> asunder . . . Whoever sees Jesus Christ
> does indeed see God and the world in
> one. He can henceforward no longer
> see God without the world or the world
> without God.
>
> Bonhoeffer, *Ethics*

SCM PRESS LTD

BLOOMSBURY STREET LONDON

FIRST PUBLISHED 1966
© SCM PRESS LTD 1966
PRINTED IN GREAT BRITAIN BY
BILLING AND SONS LTD
GUILDFORD AND LONDON

TO RUTH
the part for the whole

CONTENTS

CHAPTER ONE

Introduction: Observing the student scene

'You have one of the most fascinating jobs in the world.' It was somewhat daunting to be told that by an experienced American friend only a few months after I had started it, but it is possible to see why he said it. For I serve on the staff of the World Student Christian Federation, the body which brings together Student Christian Movements in some eighty countries, and it is the job of the staff to be in touch with what is happening in student and university circles all over the world; more particularly in my case to be in touch with what is being discussed and thought, in the hope of spotting, among the students of today, the visions of truth and commitment that may shape the world of tomorrow.

An impossible assignment, of course. In practice it appears often enough as the familiar round of a bureaucracy: sitting in committees and conferences and arranging one's own, editing publications and writing reports; but it also includes a large measure of travel, often travel to the universities of a particular country in order to bring them news from elsewhere, and, for my part, so to soak oneself in the conditions and concerns of university life there that these become a permanent factor in all the thinking and deciding in the office. Such bouts of travel are probably the most absorbing and stretching of the tasks that come my way. They provide the questions and the impulse to thought; by them provisional conclusions can be tested and revised. Since this book will smack more of those conclusions than of the background from which in fact they spring, let me begin by sketching what I found in three very different countries.

Three visits

If ever I was nearly involved in one of those turbulent demonstrations which occasionally provide the headlines of our newspapers and which express the ardent political longings and frustrations of many acute students, it was in South Korea. I happened to arrive in Seoul the day after a long series of demonstrations against the government's policies had reached their climax in a street battle with the police, a battle which the students had almost won. Martial law had been imposed at nightfall, and so I found the universities closed and army contingents camping behind sandbags and machine guns on quadrangles and tennis courts. A total ban on meetings and the sending home of all the students put paid to the programme prepared for me, and my week there had to be spent for the most part in individual conversations. The emerging picture of the country was not encouraging.

After centuries of dominance by China, the Korean people emerged from isolation at the end of the last century only to find themselves taken over by the Japanese and submitted to a harsh, alien rule which is remembered with active hatred. The final expulsion of the Japanese in 1945 coincided, however, with the division of the country, and this, not long afterwards, resulted in a civil war that brought desolation and ruin to both halves without in the end any solution to the division. Since then the southern part, supported by massive American aid, both military and civil, has known no real independence, no real wealth, no entirely trustworthy government. There are many universities but not enough jobs and openings for those who graduate to use their professional qualifications. Students are therefore intensely critical of the present conditions and regime, while having no less distaste for the alternative in the north. The dominant mood is of hopelessness and frustration. South Korea is relatively well provided, too, with Christian churches—did not Christian faith provide one of the few opportunities to speak and be Korean under the Japanese? But in these, as one might expect, there is a strong penitential emphasis, a dwelling on the vicarious suffering of Christ and on the hope of heaven hereafter which the outsider can easily dismiss as escapist but which the local conditions explain, perhaps justify.

What, in such circumstances, will be the peculiar contribution of Christian students? Surely, to seek out, point to, and themselves incarnate some signs, however humble, of confidence and hope. Perhaps it means leaving the city and accepting the poverty of village life in the hope of starting a cottage industry or co-operative which will show that the work of a few can bear fruit. Perhaps it means renouncing professional ambitions and accepting some insignificant clerkship in the hope of at least being able to do an honest and straightforward job which will counter, at one tiny point, the frustration, suspicion, and inefficiency which bedevil the whole. In any case, it will mean being utterly realist, harbouring no more illusions and no less criticism than one's fellow students, yet not despairing, not giving up, because somehow, some time, if a few at least will play their part, things will change for the better.

An almost exactly opposite situation faced me in Canada: a huge country, if with a population several millions smaller than South Korea's, becoming intoxicatingly aware of the extent of its potentialities, whether in natural resources or in international goodwill, a country with a prosperous and exciting future, unburdened as yet with the world-weariness of its great neighbour and frustrated only by various transient annoyances—the French-English divide, the dominance of American capital—which will surely be transmuted in the light of the larger purpose.

Universities are new, and bulging despite constant expansion, students lively and free in face of a world apparently wide open to them. Churches are comfortable and prosperous, if on the whole unimaginative and dull. Here, then, SCM members at their best are eager to be involved in all that is going, to explore the implications for Christian faith and for mankind of every contemporary insight and discovery, whether in biochemistry, sociology, or cybernetics, to debate with every point of view represented in the university, and to accept the sense in it without fear of syncretism, to travel all over the world in instinctive sympathy with the new and the revolutionary: in brief to try out every possibility, every available experience in an infectious if no doubt naïve optimism and self-confidence. Their fear is of any Christian self-isolation, any exclusive attitude, any complacency about the *status quo*. Perhaps they are in for a fall some day, but for the moment this would seem to be the obedience the times provide, and who will blame them for accepting it wholeheartedly?

Another very different situation, yet which has come for me to stand for the typical SCM situation in an extreme, heightened form, is that in Ethiopia. The fact that it is the one country in Africa not to have known colonial rule—the Italian occupation of 1936-41 is to be counted as a mere circumstance of war—only validates the long and proud tradition of national identity. This will change, but surely not weaken, with the rush to modernity in which, along with so many others, the nation is now absorbed. The future is admittedly uncertain, but not, for that, unpromising.

University education is very new and still confined to a small number of students, well aware of their *élite* position and of the guaranteed government salary that awaits them, whether there is an actual job for them to do or not. There is no lack of opportunity, but at the same time virtually no precedents. Students have to suffer a severe inner disorientation caused by the tension between a modern education and the traditional, almost feudal patterns of life and culture in which they have been brought up. No doubt to which pole of the tension the church belongs. Ever since King Ezana became a Christian in the fourth century, the Christian faith, with its embodiment in the (monophysite) church, has been the heart and soul of the nation, the bearer of almost all that has been distinctively Ethiopian down the centuries. The church's self-conscious apartness from other traditions of Christianity has but strengthened that bellicose defensiveness by which the country has resisted all invaders, whether Catholic Italians or Muslim Somalis. Yet that same defensiveness has resisted innovation and renewal within the church: some aspects of its life have been adapted in modern times, but the overall picture to a western eye is of a church that is still living in the fourth century and which, on any human judgement, is doomed to disappear with the advance of modernity.

Christian students, then, know the prevailing tension with particular intensity. They are scorned by most of their fellow students for bothering at all with the church in its antiquity and irrelevance. They are suspected by many in the church of following false doctrine and preaching revolt. Moreover, they are desperately short of senior friends and advisers who understand the problem and can offer appropriate experience: the few who are available are almost all foreign, and several of a different Christian tradition. Written materials are very few, in their own language non-existent. And yet the miracle continues: despite all these handicaps there exist groups of students in the various colleges who hold both to their allegiance to the church and to their modern education. To give content to that double allegiance and to bring it to bear on the development of their country are huge tasks barely begun, but those students know that this is their peculiar calling.

Who are students today?

These are but sketches of three quite distinct situations, of course not to be taken as representative of all the other places one might visit—and I must apologize to friends in these for such brutal over-simplifications. Yet in each of them the university students, not least the SCM, can be seen to have a crucial role to play within the whole network of society. We would perhaps hesitate today to call students, in the phrase of an earlier WSCF leader, 'strategic points in the world's conquest', but they remain a community which continues to deserve careful attention and which will certainly continue to draw attention to itself! It may be misleading to talk simply of 'students', since of course they are as mixed a bunch of people as any other. Some conform to a type; many do not. All the same, there are ways in which they, as a whole group, differ from other whole groups and because of which it is worthwhile for others to follow their thinking.

The reason is not that they are always outstanding people: the best, of course, are, but as the numbers of students grow, the dominant image will be that of perfectly ordinary young people who are the first to explode any false romanticism about themselves. Nor is it that they are directly aware of themselves as 'future leaders': many of the leaders of the future are likely to be university graduates, but they will not be leaders because of that fact alone, and even they were probably thinking of a quite different life while they were students. The reason for attention is rather that students, in any country and century, are those who are attentive to new ideas and eager to try them out in practice. It is not that students themselves often produce the new ideas, but that they are usually receptive to them. The ideas available may be good ones or bad ones, may come from politics, religion, psychology, art, or whatever, often all at once; may prove quite temporary or may last some generations; in any case what happens is worth watching. Society as a whole is unwise if it turns a blind eye to student experiments. The university community is thus constantly hectic, provisional, foolhardy—find what calm, adult, condescending word you like—but constantly significant.

To appreciate its significance, one must realize something of the way in which university life trains students to receive ideas. Of course, this varies with the quality of education and with the social surroundings, but the contents, methods, and results of university education are remarkably universal today, and growing more so. Two central aspects of this training can be indicated by the words 'critical' and 'functional'. Students approach things critically, not in the sense of being invariably dissatisfied with the political and educational *status quo*, though that will often result, but in the sense of an insistence on knowing for themselves the reality of any idea presented to them. They are taught to refuse to accept an assertion merely because the professor made it, and to refuse to rest content with mere repetition of the words: no doubt very few students will bring to bear the full machinery of philosophical linguistic analysis on any given assertion, but most will insist on discussion and clarification until they can accept it soberly and honestly. Further, they are trained to be aware of the objections to any assertion they may want to make, and not in fact to make it unless it can withstand these. This results in an astringent clarity that will deal harshly with many common, comfortable, but un-thought-out opinions. The same effect can be transmitted to Christians by the salutary if often shattering experience of taking a Muslim friend to share in the worship, particularly the hymn singing, of a standard, traditional Christian congregation.

The functional attitude complements the critical by insisting, in the first place, on dealing with each particular matter in the terms and within the limits that are appropriate to it. The classic instance here is that of astronomy:

even a Christian student studying the stars must do so in
terms of light waves and chemical elements, not of the
majesty and mystery of the creator. Next, it will insist on
seeing each matter under consideration in terms of its relation to the rest of human life and experience, refusing any
description, for instance, of art or intercessory prayer, that
does not tie up somehow with man's actual and practical
understanding and behaviour. It is not that each single
experience must be seen to fit into a pre-ordained whole:
the mere idea of a comprehensive and integrating frame to
knowledge is suspect for most people these days; but any
particular claim must be able to show that it has some
relevance.

Much more could be said about the origins, the presuppositions, and the limitations of such attitudes, but this is
probably enough to show that university life today, under
whatever social and ecclesiastical circumstances, provides a
severe testing to most prevalent understandings and expres-
sions of Christian faith. Faith learned in a Sunday school,
or even from a traditional catechism, will seldom by itself
hold out, except perhaps in an isolated corner of a man's
mind, and should not be able to. For the challenges the
university poses to Christian faith are the right sorts of
challenge: the challenges faith itself produces and requires,
the challenges to struggle with the living Christ through all
the complex and intricate realms of human life and thought,
in order that he may be the integrating centre of an integrated experience. Christian faith challenges to an exploration whose results cannot be certain; it commits to a risk
whose outcome one cannot see.

Thus the thinking of Christians in the university should
be at least as hectic, provisional, and foolhardy as anyone
else's—more so, perhaps, in that they include the rich
tradition of religious ideas among all the others to be
explored. This means, too, that Christians in the university
should always have much to contribute to the renewal of

the church. Given the freedom and the encouragement to experiment without inevitably involving the whole fabric of the church, they ought to be able to offer in each generation many pointers for the way ahead. Yet in practice, in the university as anywhere else, we all sooner or later turn our discoveries into securities, settle down in familiar ways, and accept all that others tell us. Christians in the university have only too often shared the tendency of the church as a whole to identify with the forms and ideas of a previous age.

A new dynamism

It was from an awareness that some such stagnation had affected many Student Christian Movements that the WSCF decided, some years ago now, on a long-term study project with the title, 'The Life and Mission of the Church'. Its aim was to regenerate among the SCMs a driving sense of purpose, a dynamic impulse to authentic Christian obedience, which would correspond in our time to the dynamic of foreign missions at the end of the last century out of which the WSCF and many of its member Movements were born. The project was launched in the belief that there were available, here and there in the church and not least in the best thinking of the ecumenical movement, insights and ideas which could re-kindle student exploration and commitment. I need not try to describe its full course. Briefly, it had two stages: a winding-up, as it were, based on a great many local and national meetings and a number of publications on the international level, leading to a world conference (at Strasbourg in 1960); and a winding-down, particularly by conferences in each continent, where the overall vision seen at its fullest in the Strasbourg conference could be explored and actualized in terms of the particular conditions of each region.

Like all such long and international studies, this one

cannot be said to have produced many neat and tidy conclusions. All along it was the purpose and framework which
mattered more than the tabulation of results. That the
people involved should be re-kindled was more important
than that a given number of 'new ideas' should be registered.
Moreover, student generations pass so quickly that it is
impossible to expect the process to move on carefully, step
by step, at the local level; it already requires a certain
distance from the immediate university scene for anyone to
be able to say what has been happening there over a period
of years. And yet, through all the conferences and publications, through all the discussions and experiments, and
through many other events and writings which happened
to coincide, one can definitely see growing a new mood, a
new direction, a new striving, which is certainly not fully
worked out yet, but which does to a great extent fulfil the
hopes invested in the project as a whole. There is indeed a
new sense of purpose abroad among Christian students,
echoing from various circles in the churches and back into
those and many more.

Let me formulate it first in quite general terms: that
Christian faith is far more closely bound up with our
experience of the world than we had thought, that Christianity can only be authentic in our day if it is a worldly
Christianity.

The phrase sounds almost contradictory, at best a paradox, because Christians have for centuries spoken of the
church and the world in terms of two different levels. It has
been assumed that there is a qualitative difference between
the two, the church being 'saved' and the world at best
waiting to be saved or condemned, at worst already condemned. It has been assumed, too, that it is the activity of
the church which is responsible for drawing the line and,
where possible, for transferring people across it. These
assumptions have been but rarely examined: those who are
Christians think and act in the framework they offer; even

those who are not, in repudiating the framework, often only turn it upside down.

Students have been discovering, not least within the WSCF's explorations, that both contemporary experience and the New Testament challenge these assumptions. Where they recognize some person or project as authentically, indisputably of Christ, it is not because they have seen men transferred from world to church, but because they have seen selfless identification with the world, unassuming service, and a deeply humble compassion. Moreover, the actual appearance and record of the church is usually all too typical of the limitations and distortions of the surrounding world; any claim of superiority which the church has established has usually led to an inhuman misuse of power. The most perceptive of Christian students feel a deep shame about much that the church has done and been. In reading the New Testament, too, they notice that while the world is often there regarded as hostile because it is estranged from God, it is the world and nothing else that is the object of God's love and purpose. The world is sinful, 'fleshly', but it is flesh that the word became; it is a new creation, not a totally other existence, which Christ's compassionate identification has brought about. John records that the church is to be in but not of the world. Yes, the church is not to be entirely limited by the world's estranged condition, but that *in* must also be given full weight: the church is not simply geographically in the world, but is to be dynamically in there in urgent solidarity, sharing fully in the world's own struggles.

We are far from the end of this rediscovery. The debate about church and world is cardinal to all else and will come up in virtually every discussion. Yet it is already clear that the cutting edge of student explorations is refusing the two-level model and is insisting that the only adequate vision is one in which God and the world are seen together, whole and finally undivided. Very often the word 'secular' is used to refer to this growing awareness, since a far-reaching and most important discussion has been unleashed by the recognition that the processes of secularization in our time have their origin partly in the event of Christ and are on the whole to be judged positively by Christians. But the more one goes into that, the less does the word 'secular' appear useful to point to the central change of heart. I have preferred here to stick to the blunter term 'worldly Christianity' in the hope that in its paradox it can truly reflect the undivided vision.

The following chapters each take up one central theme of Christian faith and life in order to point to something of what a worldly Christianity may involve there: the person of Jesus Christ, the meaning of history, the obedience of mission, worship, and the education of Christians. In each case the chapter is no more than an introduction to a contemporary debate still going on, in and beyond student circles. At times it is possible to mention insights that are finding widespread agreement, at others to suggest a conclusion that may be emerging, but all along it is a case of an open debate now more or less under way, never of one more or less rounded off. Each chapter takes a vast theme which deserves and is getting whole books to itself, and those with the time are heartily recommended to read those rather than my pages. For these contain little that is original: almost every point I have myself picked up from one place or another. My purpose here is not to track each down to its origin or to set them out duly labelled. Scholars of these discussions will look elsewhere for that. Rather I have tried, as a layman eager to understand and to see straight, to set down in my own words what seems to be arising.

But I am not only a layman: I am one who writes from a backroom and who reflects on other people's experience as much as on his own. Moreover, I have deliberately written from within the Christian tradition, hoping to provide a measure of clarity and coherence for explorations which at the time defy any set framework. A bureaucrat may hope to be of service, but if the direction this book points to is at all the right one, then it is not in the backroom or by starting from the established tradition that any real advance or any exciting discoveries will be made. These happen in the world, not in the offices of bureaucrats, however enlightened. In any domain of human thought and experience, a breakthrough is made when men bring together their grasp of reality and their driving purpose. The moon is reached as space technology is developed by the human urge to explore, and by political rivalry. So also in the history of salvation it is as Christians share in the life of the world and bring their deepest grasp of that together with the driving purpose inherent in the Christian tradition that new discoveries will be made and the world take a step or two forward.

May these chapters help us all on.

For further reading

The thinking going on within the WSCF is reflected in its quarterly journal, *Student World* (available from Annandale, North End Road, London, N.W.11; NSCF, 475 Riverside Drive, New York; or 13 rue Calvin, Geneva). See especially Nos. 1 and 4, 1963, for articles discussing some of the themes of this chapter.

CHAPTER TWO

The man behind it all: Jesus

THE impetus to explore the possibilities of a worldly Christianity usually arises from an awareness of the irrelevance of the church in the modern world; more precisely, from an awareness that the church as a whole is failing to live up to the ideas and challenges inherent in its own message. When a student appears at an SCM committee full of enthusiasm for new explorations, the chances are less that he has been brooding over his Bible than that he has been to hear a sermon or talk vibrant with first-hand experience of the struggle to live as a Christian in some acute situation, or that he has spent a month of his summer vacation redecorating houses or looking after children in an interracial slum parish. All the same, that exploration will not be able to proceed at all far without taking a careful look at the New Testament, without coming to terms with the man whose life is reported and discussed there.

Discussion about him seems to be proceeding in two at first sight utterly divergent directions. There are those, we may call them the reductionists, who seize on the fact that Jesus actually lived on earth as we do, and set about establishing as far as they can just what he was like. Only when the lumber of centuries has been cleared away, the hopes, visions, and misinterpretations that the church, however understandably in each case, has laid upon him, and his original life and personality made plain, will men be able, simply and honestly, to realize what he means today. Our generation, too, granted all the limitations that the biblical scholars have demonstrated, needs a passionate search for the historical Jesus. And so Bible study in camps and conferences is devoted particularly to the first three gospels, with perhaps an occasional glance at John in the hope that hidden in his obviously developed account may be found one or two features to add to the straightforward, human picture.

On the other hand there are those—not necessarily different people, but at least on a different tack—whose concern for the relevance of Jesus to today's world leads them to look rather into the grandiose, even exaggerated claims about him made by the early church. We may call them the enthusiasts. Our world, they know, is threatened by nuclear weapons, is in the grip of huge but mysterious economic forces, and is subject to tensions and conflicts far more dangerous than ever before; men will soon be able to take off for the moon, we have plumbed most of the workings of the human brain and are about to create life in the laboratory, we are developing international systems of security, justice, and wealth that will transform the community of mankind. To confront such a world more is needed than the straightforward human picture the reductionists are after; perhaps those wild statements Paul used to make can still have some bearing. Bible study turns to Colossians and Ephesians and struggles with the density and unevenness of Paul's writing.

Two directions, but the same search for relevance and honesty of understanding.

Unreliable documents?

A major difficulty arises immediately from the very nature of the documents to be dealt with. It is obvious that in the gospels just as much as in Paul's letters there is no 'direct' record of Jesus, but only a record that comes to us filtered through many minds. We cannot see him pure or straight. We have to accept to start from second- or umpteenth-hand materials, and to reconcile ourselves to the use of data that are not absolutely reliable.

Yet just how regrettable is this? Is it not what normally happens? We of the 1960s can only learn about Napoleon, Socrates, or Genghis Khan through a filter of human experience: the experiences of their companions, of eyewitnesses of their doings, of contemporaries writing about them, of patriots and philosophers extolling their memory, or of historians piecing together what they can from these and any other available materials. In each case the resulting record will be partial, even distorted—sometimes extremely so, sometimes so little that we do not notice it; it is never pure or straight. Even in the case of contemporary events and people, we rely for most of our information on journalists and biographers who, for all their possible concern for impartiality and accuracy, cannot but select and condition in one way or another their 'raw material'. Further yet, the events and people we ourselves directly experience do not come to us as they are 'in themselves': it is a commonplace of philosophy and the natural sciences nowadays to say that the implicit structures of the human mind, let alone variables such as an individual's temperament and the conditions of his upbringing, influence our reception of what we experience. This is not the place to pursue an extremely intricate—and far from finished—philosophical discussion about human knowledge, but it is obvious that we should have no false expectations about what it is possible to know of the man Jesus. It belongs already to a worldly interpretation that we accept to receive report of him, as in fact we do, from the experience of others.

Moreover, the authors of the New Testament would never have claimed to be presenting any absolutely pure record. They knew perfectly well, as the prefaces Luke set at the head of his gospel and of Acts say deliberately, that what

they were writing down was a crystallization of a whole
tradition of memory, speculation, and devotion. Its diverse
elements were to be found in the more or less general teachings of the many communities of Christians, and in the
minds and mouths of particular individuals. These writers
were not creating the tradition, but trying to put it straight,
to make sense of it; and even if this involved their including
some points and phrases from their own effort to make sense
rather than from anyone else's, they knew themselves to
stand within the same tradition and believed their interpretation faithful to it.

In our own time, biblical scholars have reached understandings of the processes of the writings of the New Testament which help us to be relatively sure that that tradition,
for all its diversity and richness already by the time the
epistles and gospels came to be written down, is indeed
largely based on the experience of those who actually knew
Jesus. Of course, that experience was developed and re-
interpreted in the light of what happened later. Even the
gospels, which quite deliberately look back to the period
before the church as such existed, are clearly documents of
the church; they can only be understood with some knowledge of what did in fact later happen in and to that
church. Yet with the available results of scholarship—and
for all the variety, complexity, and dexterity of New Testament scholarship to one who approaches it for the first time,
there are results which can readily be available—and with
normal human sensitivity and imagination it is quite possible to overcome the stumbling-blocks inherent in the
nature of the material and recapture much of the original
experiences that gave rise to the tradition. If we know we
are seeking a worldly understanding that will necessarily
rely on the experience of others, for all their limitations,
and if we renounce expectations of something supernatural,
miraculous, and utterly special, then whether we follow the
reductionists in looking for the man of Nazareth or the

enthusiasts in looking for the Lord of the universe, we can find quite a lot of sense.

(A Christian evangelist once told me: 'When I'm talking to Muslim students I talk about the virgin birth, the miracles, and the resurrection: that puts them on the track.' Perhaps, but it is a track that will probably alienate them for life from knowledge of the living Christ! Some Christians may want to retain the terms supernatural, miraculous, and special, but if so let it be because these are the only adequate vehicles to convey what began as a definite, worldly, human experience.)

The Jesus of history

Let us first follow the reductionists, asking how the man Jesus struck his original followers. The outline of the story is fairly clear. People began to take notice of Jesus in the setting of the revivalist preaching of John, known as the Baptist. Later Jesus was to tell his disciples that it was his baptism by John that launched him into his own particular calling, but at first he seemed much like others affected by that movement. (Later still, memories and meditations stored up in the circles close to Jesus' own family—cf. Luke's account—and legends and speculations taking up themes and pointers from the Old Testament—cf. Matthew's account—came to lay the initial and basic stress on the manner and fact of his birth. Whatever the significance of these, it is clear that for the first followers the story started with John and his activities.)

Soon Jesus, too, took up a life of itinerant preaching, mainly in Galilee, during which he became known especially for his powers of healing, powers that were successful with both physical and mental illnesses, but which he himself considered secondary to his preaching about the rule of God. Any special powers he had, he kept on stressing to the disciples, were no more than signs of the truth of his preaching that this rule, this kingdom, was about to begin, indeed was already beginning with his own presence among them. It was urgent that people realize the importance of this, wake up out of their old habits, and be prepared to accept and enter into it. Not only did he himself preach this message; he actively recruited others to help him preach. Some came and asked to be enrolled in the company, but others, among them some who came to be leaders, he sought out for himself, as they had cause to remember, with an imperious command that they leave occupation and family and join his band.

His free, unconventional, and indeed arrogant handling of the carefully regulated ethico-religious requirements of the Jewish culture brought him into some unpopularity with the Jewish religious authorities, and while he made no overt act against the Roman occupation, the turbulence he brought into the Jews' affairs must already have made him politically suspect too. It took some courage, therefore, to decide, as he did, to go up to the Passover feast at Jerusalem one year, but he made no effort to do it secretly; there was even a demonstration in his favour as he arrived. He continued to preach in the city, but the authorities, particularly the Jewish High Priest and Council, were increasingly vexed by him and eventually decided that he must be done away with. They suborned one of the inner circle of his followers. And from then on it only took a certain amount of unlovely machinations, initiated by the Jewish authorities but in which the Romans were also involved, and he was put to death by crucifixion just before the actual feast.

What sort of a man was he? Obviously *a fascinator*. He fascinated the twelve for all their failure to understand what he was about, and through them he fascinates us, either in his favour or against him. Just as all the characters in the gospels who come near him are drawn into an opinion or a decision one way or the other, so in our own time we can find those who like what they know of him and those who reckon him a source of error and harm. What is hard to imagine is the man who, having read the documents with care and with an awareness of the sort of documents they are, finishes by saying, 'I can't say I find anything very striking there at all; it merely leaves me cold.'

His fascination is not that of a schizophrenic: in his own, clearly rich and complex way, he strikes one as *an integrated personality*. Unpredictable, perhaps, but not inconsistent: a man with a steady purpose. The gospels tend to portray him knowing exactly what he wanted and what would happen to him from his baptism on, but that is no doubt a rationalization; we can imagine that, even in the experience of the twelve, his purpose grew and became more precise over the months they knew him. Yet that which grew was recognizably the same purpose: he never changed direction even if it was not at all clear to the others exactly what that direction was.

He was *singularly unselfish*, knowing how to make himself available to others, to identify with them, to live in solidarity with them, always at the service of those around him— though he had his own conceptions of what the appropriate service was. He lived, as has been said, 'for others,' not for himself. And he lived for *all* others in a society that knew its share of social barriers. He seemed to make a point of going to help the lepers and the madmen, the outcasts of Jewish society; of being together with the taxgatherers, usually despised for their acceptance of the Roman regime and for the way they turned it to profit; or of talking to and about Samaritans, the almost hereditary enemies of the Jews because of their heretical teachings and practices. In none of these cases did he make a theory out of it, at least not to his disciples. He simply lived and acted as he saw fit, showing by that alone that social barriers were purely man-made and secondary to the overriding purpose. To be sure, he insisted for reasons connected with the rule he preached on restricting his work to the Jewish people (presumably including the Samaritans), but he was prepared to enlarge his practice even there when human solidarity required.

At the same time, there was *a remarkable bluntness and directness* about the way he approached other people. The disciples remembered him saying exactly what he thought, however odd, disconcerting, or even upsetting. The equivalent of this in his teaching was a constant note of authority that came not from great learning or from faithfulness to another source recognized to be authoritative, but quite simply from his own manner and teaching. He was apparently setting himself up as a sufficient authority—and people again and again recognized him to be so. In virtue of his directness and authority he was always facing people with a decision whether to accept him or not, sometimes quite explicitly by a question or a challenge, sometimes in more veiled terms by telling a parable which in fact referred to the situation in which it was told, sometimes again purely by being the man he was and so implicitly challenging the securities by which men lived. Some people, on the whole the poor, the needy, and the unassuming, found in him an unexpected promise of acceptance and hope for a better life; others, on the whole the well-off and the self-satisfied, found him an intolerable threat to the life they had built for themselves.

He was a man *open*, not only to other men and women, but also to the whole range of life. Nobody could be less of a specialist. He would use illustrations from nature, from farming, from social life, like any village storyteller, and combine them with quite precise insight into the political circumstances and with a full mastery of the religious heritage of his people. Further, he was open to what each passing moment would bring, always indeed busy with other people, with his followers, with his prayers, but in such a way that he could be carefree and serene, without worry, unless at the failure of his followers to understand what he meant—though as they looked back after the point where understanding had come to them, they remembered him being cheerful even about their incomprehension.

By the same token, his openness made him *vulnerable*, but he refused to take measures to protect himself, whether from the sick thronging to be healed, the listening crowd who might blame him for their hunger or, in the end, from the disciple who betrayed him. He let things happen, confident either in his own ability to master the situation or in the overriding care and purpose of him whom he called father. Even the haunting cry from the cross, 'My God, my God, why hast thou forsaken me?', is at least to be taken as an indication of his openness to that father in a moment of extremity, when his own heart and mind were no longer sure of the relationship. It is thus an implicit and paradoxical affirmation of the very certainty and praise to which the Psalm it comes from arrives in the end.

His teaching was always fresh but seldom very original; much of it could be found in one form or another in the Jewish scriptures. The disciples came to see eventually, as they then realized he had often hinted, that his teaching was to be understood as but the expression, like his healings and his social contacts, of who he was. What really mattered was that it was he who was teaching it. And what made him what he was was *his relationship with 'the father'*. Again and again when talking about his purposes he would point beyond himself to the father, and the disciples remembered him making frequent occasion for solitary prayer. It was to be presumed that by his 'father' he was referring to God, the God of Israel known and celebrated through the Jewish scriptures, but when pressed for an explanation about the father he would only refer to himself! At the same time, despite this apparently high valuation of himself, he was careful to disclaim any particular status or title by which people could place or value him. The disciples obviously cherished memories of the time when they first acknowledged him by the title that was to stick: the Anointed, the

Christ, but they remembered in the same breath his command not to use this title and his refusal to use it himself.

To sum up this sketch of the reductionist enquiry, we may say, with a word that seems to find a particular echo in our own day, that he was a man who appeared to others to be extraordinarily *free*. Negatively, he was free *from* personal anxiety and insecurity, from the social patterns and restraints of the prevailing ethico-religious culture—free from anything that stood in the way of his living in the way he thought man was meant to live, to the extent—at least in the disciples' later memories—of being free from some of the usual limitations of humankind : they remembered him walking on water and stilling a storm. Yet it is clear that he was not free from the entreaties and threats of his fellow men, nor from death. Positively, he was free *for* his neighbour, for his people as a whole, for the relationship with his father, for the calling and purpose he knew to be supremely urgent and important. The limits of his own freedom were set by the freedom of others; the purpose of his freedom was the greater freedom of others.

The central question

But this is to jump ahead. So far we have been outlining the possible findings of a reductionist, sifting the experience of the disciples for a portrait of the man Jesus as he lived: an unusual, enigmatic man even to his own family and followers, but still nothing but a man. History knows other enigmas. History knows other men who lived in solidarity with their people, who had an intrinsic authority, who were extraordinarily free. While they lived with him the disciples would have said only that it was their good fortune to have fallen in with this one. The claim they were to launch, the claim that he was different from and more than all others, rests on their later experience and only on their knowledge of him as they meditated on and interpreted this in the light of that later experience. Here we come to the central point of any enquiry about Jesus, the question of the resurrection. Students of today are not the first to find this incredible, but they do, and if they can make sense of it at all it is by an insistence on understanding the origin of this teaching. At this point especially, Christians must talk realistically and straight.

The disciples were shattered by Jesus' death. They had entrusted their hopes and their lives to him and now he was gone. We know no details, but we can well imagine their state. And then some weeks later, it may even have been a matter of days, they were out in the streets proclaiming a triumphant message based on the fact that Jesus had come back to them. It is impossible to know exactly what they said: the sermons retailed in Acts are at best a reconstruction. But from all that we read in the epistles and all that we know of the presuppositions of the gospels, it is clear that the message of the resurrection is basic to every stage of Christian preaching and teaching. The actual stories we have of the resurrection certainly owe a good deal to later thought and embroidery; it would be a wise and courageous man indeed who would undertake to sort out 'fact' from 'fiction' in them. Indeed, that is the wrong question with which to approach them. What matters is not that the stone had indeed been moved or that the risen Jesus did actually light a fire to cook the breakfast on. What matters is that the disciples said with conviction and joy that he had come back to them and that this was enough to turn them from frightened country fishermen into men who could set in motion the whole history of the church and thus of the modern world.

The 'fact' of the resurrection is not the 'fact' of Jesus' leaving the grave but the 'fact' of the disciples' preaching a message based on the assertion of his return to them, and this 'fact' seems to be historically unassailable. Into the experience that lies behind it we cannot penetrate at all far.

We can only verify their assertion by making our own judgement of the appropriateness and consistency of their subsequent actions and motives. Did they live and behave as men to whom their leader and teacher had returned after death? Again, a yes is the more appropriate and possible answer. Beyond that it is not unreasonable to accept that, in general terms (for some details are undoubtedly misleading), the stories which came to be preserved are based upon and reflect the original experience of the disciples. The vital points seem to have been these: that it was the same man who came back; that it was he who appeared, not they who conjured him up; that his appearing was connected with a meal, just as a meal had rounded off his previous life with them; that he came with authority and commissioned them to preach and teach in his name in continuance of his own commission; and that after a time he came back no more.

From then on, too, it is impossible to follow the thoughts and experiences of the disciples in any detail, but the book of Acts offers a framework which is, overall, quite realistic and possible. As a result of their experience of the risen Jesus, they enthusiastically and wholeheartedly proclaimed him as the Messiah, the Anointed of God, the fulfilment of the hopes of Israel. This is to say that their message involved a re-interpretation and re-presentation of Israel's understanding of her own history which took up and clarified what Jesus had been talking about, often mysteriously, in his teaching on God's rule.

The Jewish people were expecting, indeed yearning for a last day in which God would appoint a ruler for them and usher in the age of peace and perfection. Perhaps at first the disciples thought that the resurrection had shown that this Ruler, when he eventually came, would be Jesus. Even if so, it cannot have been long before they came to what remains the central Christian affirmation, that the resurrection shows that Jesus already *is* the ruler. The last day has come; the communication with God broken by man's self-centredness

B

has been restored by the perfect openness of one man; the Spirit of God responsible for the creation of the world and the preservation of Israel has now been made available to the disciples and through them to all who believe; the whole world is to be told of the triumph and faithfulness of God. We can see the disciples ransacking the Jewish scriptures and the images of contemporary expectation for means of describing and conveying the overwhelming meaning of what had happened to them in and because of Jesus. They throw themselves enthusiastically into their task, even if they have very little idea of what it is going to involve.

Before so very long, perhaps some fifteen years after Easter, there must have been circulating in the church conceptions of Jesus that were magnificent and grandiose in the extreme, incorporating images and symbols from the Jewish scriptures and elsewhere to assert his primacy and glory. He is higher than all the angels; he has saved not only Israel but all men, not only men but the whole creation; his work can never be undone; God has made him ruler and judge; he is the son of God—he *is* God. Speculation had plenty of models and precedents in other faiths with which to play, and was not loth to do so. The enthusiasts of the time went all out. Much of what came to be believed and said about Jesus was indeed speculation and dangerously far removed from the astonishing but perfectly real experience of the disciples.

This must have occupied Paul a great deal, for part of what we owe to him is a careful and reasonable teasing out of what can be and is to be said. Like the first disciples, he based his preaching on an assertion of experience of the risen Jesus, so that behind his words we can sense reflection on experience and not mere speculation. But it was the risen Jesus he had known, not Jesus during his human life, and so his concern is less aligned with that of those we have called the reductionists than with that of the enthusiasts. Of the various letter-writers whose works came to be recognized as authoritative, it is Paul who provides the fullest pictures and whose writings must be explored if sense is to be made of the church's traditional belief in Jesus the Lord, Son of God, and Saviour of all. What sort of a man is this?

The Christ of faith

In the first place, we find the assertion that it is he who is *the ruler*, he who is in charge of the universe. It is no longer any blind fate or any unknown power which, behind and beyond the actions of men, controls what will and does happen, but this same Jesus. The early Christians could not, of course, prove such a claim; it is not the kind of thing that can be proved. All you can do is to judge whether, given the people who make it, it is at all worth entertaining and trying out. In making it, the Christians were expressing their conviction that in the risen Jesus they had met the *end* of the world, in the sense of its perfection and goal, and that not as any static ideal but as the person who was actively engaged in bringing the world to that end.

At the same time they talked of the ascension. The details of the story in which they recorded it obscure for us their intention, but if we think of their experience then they must have wanted to point to the fact that Jesus' rule is *hidden*. They knew that he had gone away and was no longer appearing to them or to those who believed in him through their words—no wonder Paul found acceptance slow. But this did not invalidate his rule and his work: it only meant that men were not to be able to see it but would have to risk committing themselves to it in faith, despite the ordinariness, the humility, and the ambiguity of his earthly life and of the church. The overwhelming certainty that despite all appearances it is this man who is in charge was only given once in the physical terms of a risen body, but once was enough.

This image of Jesus ruling will not often prove meaningful in our day. We know too much about human freedom and responsibility and too much about the evil power of superstition to take it at all literally. To think of a 'hidden ruler' is to conjure up quite the wrong sort of picture. But to be uneasy with their terms need not lead us to reject their message. The notion of *coherence* offers one element: the observable fact that for all its variety and freedom the world does hold together; and that of *finality* another: the fact that the world is going somewhere, is moving in what future historians will be able to see as a dominant direction. Coherence and finality, as concepts, are both dynamic, not merely descriptive, and also personal, in that we know the deepest meaning of each not in terms of nature or even of technology, but in terms of human personality. Taken together and referred to the man Jesus, they come close to saying what the disciples meant in calling him Lord.

In a similar metaphor the early church maintained that the risen Jesus is the *judge*, or more precisely is *the judge's trusted pleader*, standing on the right-hand side of the court, whose word for or against a man is judgement enough. Here they were taking up an image from the Jewish scriptures to express the conviction that what ultimately matters for each one of us and for the world as a whole is the way we take a stand in line with or contrary to the driving purpose and intention of the man Jesus. Again, the ascension means that this judgement is hidden. Men are not to be able to distinguish between him who is accepted and him who has shut himself out. Nor can we pretend to know exactly how the process works—in an age when we are so well aware of the pressures of society it can probably be agreed that the metaphor of the individual up for trial is no longer fully adequate. But the resurrection gave the conviction that it is no social norm, no religiously sanctioned law, no party line, no human achievement that ultimately matters, but only the sanction of Jesus.

To say that he is the ruler and the advocate involved the

further claim that *he has conquered the powers*, all those forces, known or unknown, which influence and control things as they are. At the time of the early church men believed in a whole hierarchy of these unseen but potent beings, but Jesus' freedom from death confirmed for the disciples the evidence of his healings that any such powers were subordinate to him. The powers remained active, and often malignant, because that was the way the world was, but this one man had shown his superiority to them, and so they were already in principle overcome. In our day we no longer talk of 'powers and principalities', but we do know and talk of many forces from which, once we have eyes to see, we long for ourselves and others to be free—the forces of nature in earthquake and typhoon, the forces of disease and old age, the forces of tradition and social conditioning, economic forces, political forces, even the forces of religion. These need no reinterpretation, and the message that freedom from them is possible can still ring out as good news.

More than that, the resurrection demonstrated that in him there was available the possibility of *communication with God*. Man's estrangement from the source and ground of all that is, which the Jews had so profoundly described in the story of Adam's choosing to be responsible for himself, was now overcome. For Jesus had all along refused to be responsible for himself; he had made himself completely open and available to his neighbour and to his father and had let happen to him what would. That he was not the product of chance nor lost in an alien universe, but had genuinely been in touch with the ultimate was now shown by the resurrection. Moreover, this communication was made available to the disciples in the gift of what they came to call the Spirit, namely the power, the personality, the confidence that had been Jesus' in his lifetime and which was now to ensure communication between himself and men. For the Spirit was not limited to the original disciples. They were in turn to make this gift available to others, and

those others to others down the centuries. The world,
through some of its members, is now in communication
with the pleader and represented in his positive advocacy—
a fundamental promise of enduring significance for men's
transitory lives.

This is clearly a matter of faith, not sight, as must be any
other claim to be in contact with the ultimate. And it is
clear that even the enthusiastic first disciples knew that more
had to happen before the fullness of communication would
be available; we in turn would have to be raised from the
dead, for instance. But already now communication is established in one man, and in him the whole of each man, the
whole of mankind, and indeed, through man, the whole of
the universe has the chance to move towards and into the
perfection of all that they are and can be. Of course, men
can and do continue in their self-centredness and so refuse
the possibility for themselves, each other, and the universe
entrusted to them, and of course the church misunderstands
and disobeys its calling, but we have seen openness and communication available in one man and know from him that
no one and nothing is categorically excluded.

This involves the further claim that health and wholeness
are to be found in him and, beyond that, that he is *the
representative man*, the forerunner and type of what we all
can be. And not only of what we may become, but of what
we were all along intended to be. As they pursued this kind
of idea, the early church—with Paul and John as their
spokesmen—came to the belief that Jesus was the centre
and purpose of the whole world, not only now but also from
its original creation, that he is not only the end but also the
beginning of history. In other words, Jesus comes to be seen
as the manifestation of God, not only in his lifetime for his
contemporaries, not only after his resurrection for men of
future ages, but even for the entire creation since the beginning. They come to see not only that all things are now
moving towards fulfilment in him, but also that all things

always have been; they come to see the original purpose of
creation in him, and talk of God creating the worlds 'by
him'. Jesus is not only 'post-existent' in the resurrection, but
is seen as pre-existent 'before all worlds'.

Because of this we inherit the prevalent picture of Jesus as
the one who 'came down' from heaven and then went back,
a picture which is often used to deny his manhood and
which saps the resurrection of its distinctive excitement and
promise. Pre-existence as some sort of 'fact' is neither com-
prehensible nor significant. What matters is the implicit
claim that this man is the criterion and goal, not only of
Jewish history and religion, but of every history, every hope,
every faith that has ever been. Any kind of natural religion,
or any striving after perfection, truth, beauty, moral obedience or freedom, whether seen in terms of a god or not—he
is who you were after. If ever you thought you had seen
something of the 'really real', it is by him that you can now
test it and be sure. This all-embracing assertion, still just as
unusual, as controversial, and as relevant as ever, is but the
furthest working out of the experience of the resurrection.

These are the kind of claims which the enthusiasts explore
and echo. They are certainly high-sounding and exuberant
in a way that the findings of the reductionists are not, but it
need not be said that they are totally 'supernatural' and thus
meaningless; in their own way they are worldly claims too.
In the first place they arise from the experience of the disciples, not from some religious void. Theirs was admittedly
a startlingly unusual experience, but they were quite ordinary and human people who had it. But also in our case, we
who hear and have to test these claims, they speak to our
worldly experience or not at all. They are claims not for
some merely supernal status of Jesus in himself, but for
him as he acts on and within our familiar universe. They
are claims for his function in history: that he is in charge of
it, that he is the final test of what is worth while, that he
makes possible and actual what could be mere concepts such

as truth, justice, value, and meaning, that he makes known the perfection of humankind, and all these in an active, dynamic sense that makes him the chief agent of history as well as its goal. What this means we shall explore further in the next chapter, but at least these claims, however they have to be qualified and expounded, can be seen to refer to human experience.

The same man

But above all these are worldly claims because they talk of the same man as the disciples had known in Galilee and Jerusalem. Their resurrection message proclaimed no disembodied ghost, but the man Jesus in the flesh. He was more than he had been—his freedom had now conquered the limitations of death—but every bit as human and real. And he acted in the same ways, by attracting and fascinating people—his biblical lecture on the road to Emmaus must at least have avoided being boring for the two strangers to invite him in—but without forcing himself on anyone. His refusal of the temptations to impose awareness of his power remains as complete as before. He does nothing to overrule human freedom since his purpose is to increase and perfect it. The victor who rose remains the one who died in putting up with the worst which others could do to him. No wonder that John, writing out of the most developed tradition to be found in the New Testament and whose gospel reflects a very full meditation on both the original experience of the disciples and the later experiences of the church, sees Jesus' vulnerability and his triumph coinciding on the cross. It is not, for John, that the humiliation of being crucified is succeeded by the victory of being resurrected, but that the low point of innocent and representative suffering is by being so the height of victory and majesty. Jesus being who he in fact is, and our universe being what it in fact is, these are not two but one.

Thus in the end the two explorations we have followed converge and belong together. On the one hand we have a human Jesus, on the other a cosmic Christ, the one individual, modest, and vulnerable, the other universal, grandiose, and demanding. But these are only the polar accents of the same man, who in all his aspects refers to our own human being. Because his humanity went beyond their own, the disciples took him for their goal and ideal and invite us to do likewise, but it is our humanity of which he is the goal. We may not say: the man of Nazareth, however unusual, can at least be grasped, whereas the cosmic Christ is just incomprehensible. Perhaps this is the way it strikes us at first, but in fact the one leads to the other; both are equally human, i.e., if we will allow our conception of humanity to be stretched by him. The man of Nazareth can be seen in terms of the world we know, but points beyond it; the cosmic Christ is to be seen in terms of the world as it will be at the end, but which he is already developing towards its perfection. Nor may we say: we can know something of the man Jesus through the experience of the disciples, whereas to know the cosmic Christ we have to have recourse to some special category of 'religious' experience. No, it is equally through the experience of the disciples that we know of the cosmic Christ; it is equally in the worldly realities of history and other people that we can look for evidence that might confirm their claims.

The two explorations also complement and correct one another. If we concentrate on the man of Nazareth our findings are likely to be of a striking teacher whose words still have power to surprise and move us. What we shall miss is the certainty of victory and the universal scope of his action. If we concentrate on the cosmic Lord we may be caught up in enthusiastic affirmations about the end of history, but we shall run the risk of losing touch with the real world and falling into a totalitarian attitude; we shall need to remember the human solidarity of Jesus with all men in their freedom, and his vulnerable openness to others, however they reacted to him. By holding to the entire range of conceptions of him found in the New Testament, we are both being true to the disciples' original experience of him and to the scope inherent in any search for an adequate basis for living in today's world.

For further reading

Above all, the New Testament, with the fresh look a modern translation affords. Then two books from which most of this chapter has been covertly cribbed: *The Secular Meaning of the Gospel* by Paul van Buren (Macmillan, New York, and SCM Press, London), and *Jesus of Nazareth* by Günther Bornkamm (Harper and Row, New York, and Hodder and Stoughton, London).

CHAPTER THREE

Where are we headed?: History

ONE day I found myself sitting at table with two others, a clergyman and a student. The student was explaining the problem he had about Christian belief. He had been to church services often enough and to many a meeting discussing Christianity; he had read a good deal about it all and knew more or less what Christian thinkers had to say, but as far as he himself was concerned he just did not know whether he was a Christian or not, and was not sure how he could find out. What had we to say about that? And so, one after the other, the pastor and I tried to say something that might help him to know. I noticed that we followed rather different tracks.

'Have you ever known what it is to be accepted?' the pastor said (or words to this effect). 'Have you ever fallen out of relationship with someone and then been surprised to find him continuing to accept you, willing to carry on the relationship and let it grow despite what had come between you? The Christian is one who knows himself accepted by the father of Jesus Christ despite all that he is and does which disturbs that relationship.' I, on the other hand, found myself saying, 'You used to study sociology but have now switched to psychology. What was your reason for doing so? What purpose do you see in studying at all? How do you see your aims for yourself fitting in with your expectations and hopes for the world as a whole? The Christian is one who finds the governing purpose both for his own life and for the whole world in Jesus Christ, and who tries to shape his life accordingly.'

We were following two of the classic tracks of Christian apologetics, the one concentrating on the individual's personal assurance of his own salvation, of his acceptance by God despite human sin and inadequacy; the other looking to the meaning of history and to the individual's own place and purpose within that larger framework. Now it is no part of my purpose in this chapter to decry the first of these approaches and to insist that I was right. As I remember the incident, the student did not consider himself much helped by either of us, and in any case a single meal is hardly long enough for strangers to know one another to the point where they can really share in the answering of such a question. My point in recounting it is rather to show that discussion of the value and reality of Christian faith need not be centred on the more or less psychological experience of many individuals, but can proceed in terms of the quite ordinary decisions each of us makes.

The world is undergoing in our time a dynamic process of change and upheaval for the scope and speed of which history can offer few parallels. Students, whose daily experience in common room and laboratory continually faces them with insights and decisions their parents know virtually nothing of, can make sense of life only as they see it subject to change. The process of change is not only rapid but universal, since it is clear that the fate of each one of us depends on things that may happen at any time in any part of the earth. A worldly Christianity is therefore bound to find itself struggling with history—history in the sense not only of what is now past but of the fact that everything moves on from one stage and condition to the next. A worldly faith must have no lesser dimensions than the world it refers to.

This is, moreover, no reluctant adaptation to the contemporary spirit. For the Christian gospel is essentially a message about history. To talk about what is going on in our world is to stand on ground where we Christians have something to offer. And it is to stand on ground of equal interest to those who do not share our loyalty. The future of Kenya or Indonesia is of burning interest to all students there, whatever their faith or political opinion. Only as Christians know how to wrestle with the meaning of our time can Christianity decisively leave behind the ghetto of private 'religion' and public irrelevance.

The biblical framework

The way we can discuss any one segment of contemporary history will never be taken straight from the Bible, for the Bible is not about our contemporary history in any straightforward sense. The Bible is concerned with a segment of history far removed from our own, namely that of the Jewish people between, roughly, 1200 BC and AD 100. It records their history, admittedly in a most disjointed and confused way, and yet also records the understanding of that history held by a long line of people who came to be accepted as those standing in the true tradition of interpretation: the Old Testament by the leaders of the Jews some time after they returned from exile, and the New, along with the Old, by the leaders of the Christian church after its first period of growth. That tradition, taken as a whole, offers an understanding of that particular segment of history which it at the same time affirms to be true for the history of all. It is by taking over the biblical framework of interpretation that Christians may find meaning in each new age.

The biblical writers deliberately wrote about their own history and in its terms, and there are all sorts of diversities among them, some enriching, some confusing; no wonder we in our time have to make an effort to find much sense, let alone relevance, in it. Yet contemporary developments and pressures are not only helping us to understand more accurately and vividly the original intention and meaning of the Bible by providing tools of scholarship such as archaeology and literary criticism; they can be seen to vindicate the peculiar framework the Bible has to offer.

The framework basic to the Old Testament is that of history stretching from the creation to the last day. Of that which lies beyond these limits nothing can be known. What is known is history, and it is known by the Jews as the responsibility of that power (presence, name, agent—our modern categories just do not fit) they called God. He began all things at the beginning, and he will end them one day. Between these two poles he has chosen one particular people and nation to have knowledge of him and to be the sign of his activity over all the world. And so the Jewish prophets interpreted the history of their people as the history of God's signs to the world. They had no very constant idea of what the end they were moving towards would be, yet at least it would be no mere arbitrary breaking off, but the fulfilment of whatever it was God intended for the whole world.

This remains the overall framework for the New Testament also, but with the vital change that the end of history, in the sense of the fulfilment of God's intentions, is no longer identified with the temporal finish but is affirmed to have already taken place in that event which was the whole happening of Jesus the Christ. History is no longer one single period but two: from the creation to Jesus, and from Jesus to the end. No longer do the extremities define the purpose of history, as if man or the whole world were defined by the way he was created to be or by what he was to become; man is now defined by the centre of history, by that particular man; indeed both the creation and the end are affirmed to have their meaning in him.

This shift between the testaments involves a quite particular way of regarding the second period, the one in which we still live. History is not yet at an end, but its fulfilment—the highest realization of what was intended in creation and the perfection towards which it moves—has already happened and can be known in the man Jesus. The New Testament affirms that the fulfilment has happened and is known in one man; it remains to happen and be known over the whole world. The fulfilment, to stretch our terminology, needs its completion. Thus in all that the New Testament writers have to say about the present there is a holding in tension of that which *already* is and that which is *yet to come*, and this is what gives a quite distinctive flavour to the Christian understanding of history.

It could sound as if all this is said about some part or essence of our human lives, about that 'soul' with which 'religion' deals but which for the purposes of normal living we can and do forget about entirely. But no: these claims about history are indeed about our normal living within history and have no purpose or sense if they do not refer to that. It is precisely the history which is made up of wars, strikes, and elections, or of cooking, work at the office, and trips away in the car at weekends—the whole of it, however apparently transient or trivial—which is already fulfilled but remains to be worked out and seen to be complete.

It could sound, too, as if this is all automatic, as if history naturally moves onwards and upwards, and things get better and better all the time. No, for the New Testament always stresses the freedom and responsibility of man: he can choose to impose his own purpose or to release the purpose of Jesus. All the imperfections of the world that mark its estrangement—whether deserts, diseases, dictators or death —are now in principle overcome in Jesus. Men, by appropriating the communication he makes available, can find the ways of subduing them. But they can also turn those ways to their own advantage, and on their showing up to now are likely to do this most of the time. The terms 'good' and 'evil' are not labels to be applied to particular things in themselves, but point to different ways in which men can help history move on. Thus human life in history, as long as history remains, will never be free from moral choices. The movement towards the fulfilment will never be free of blockages and reversals.

One New Testament image in which much of this is summed up is that of *the resurrection of the body*. This has become part of the church's often incomprehensible jargon, but needs to be seen anew in terms of its meaning for our history. Jesus was restored to his disciples not as a soul or spirit, but precisely in his own body. They remembered him coming and going with disconcerting suddenness, even through closed doors, but they also remembered him eating with them and letting them feel his scars. Perhaps we are to conclude that the risen Jesus had even more physical capacities than ordinary men, but at least he had all we have. This is not an assertion about the actual molecules of his particular flesh : it is impossible to say scientifically 'what happened' to him, let alone what will to us, in that respect. But our inevitable question at that point does not invalidate the experience of the disciples—and if their claim that this man is ultimately in charge of all things is true, we need not insist on stumbling over his capacity to do strange things with molecules : we are beginning to do some ourselves ! The point of emphasizing his resurrection in the *body* lies in the promise implicit in it.

It offers a promise in the first instance to mankind. Since this one man had conquered death, his followers proclaimed, no one need now fear it. Those who would believe and be baptized into the community of believers would share in the body of Christ since they lived his life, not their own, and could rely even now on the promise of eventual resurrection. But the promise is not only to them; it is addressed to all men. The body of Christ is intrinsically universal. At the end of history that promise will be universally accepted and the head will be followed by the entire body.

Further, the resurrection of the body contains a promise to the whole natural order, including the molecules. In the Old Testament, man is seen to have the capacity of using and dominating the rest of nature. This capacity extends in the New Testament into that of transforming nature into the new creation, the fulfilment of the original creation. And indeed, the longer history continues the more we see already and can expect to see in the future man's reshaping of nature. Usually he does it to suit himself, but often enough his reshaping can seem to foreshadow that final state of things seen in the vision of John of Patmos as the New Jerusalem. This is, significantly, a city, a human artefact, no 'natural' paradise. The recreation of nature will happen through man, as he works out the promise of the resurrection.

The resurrection of Jesus only came after the suffering on the cross. The believer's acceptance of the promise involves the renunciation of self and the willingness to assume the suffering of the world. The new creation, too, will involve no little pain; we need not expect to move uninterruptedly towards the goal. The City comes down from heaven and is not simply like Babel, to be built upon earth. Yet what men do on earth contributes to it, and life in the new age is recognizably worldly, only more so.

At the same time, the resurrection of the body is primarily a promise and no blueprint for the future. The New Testament does not try to specify, any more than the Old, exactly what things will be like at the end, let alone at any point on the way to it. All visions and speculations boil down to the basic certainty that the end will be no more than the working out of what has already been seen in Jesus. Indeed, one constant strand is that of a rejection of speculation in favour of a concentration on living out the present, open and expectant towards the future, and obedient to that which already is and can be known.

The resurrection, then, stresses again that the line of history has turned at its centre. It is not just a single movement, as teachings about evolution might imply. Nor is it an endlessly recurring, circular movement as in some fatalist teachings. It has turned and is going somewhere. This notion of a centre to history is interesting not only for history as a whole but also for each of us within it. What do we live from, on what basis? What do we live towards, with what hope? Where those two questions converge our present lives are lived. And both the Christian dares to answer with the name and person of Jesus.

The contemporary scene: the strong points

So much—and it can only be a rapid outline—for the framework of understanding offered in the Bible. We must now turn to our own contemporary history and see what, if anything, to be observed there at all confirms these expectations. Christian students are increasingly discovering that there are indeed points of confirmation to be found and that these ought to be central to the vision and obedience of the church. But one must specify quite deliberately and carefully: first, that we cannot expect any proofs by which to convince ourselves, let alone others, that the framework the Bible offers is obviously true; all we can expect are pieces of evidence which seem to confirm the hypothesis the Bible offers; and, second, that we must openly and honestly deal with the realities of our contemporary history, resisting the temptation to concentrate on favourable appearances or to idealize what merely might be. In this exercise the Christian will often enough arrive at conclusions different in one way or another from those of the Marxist, the Muslim, or the man who claims to stand in no particular tradition, but he must at least be seen to be dealing with the same world and the same history as they do.

Let us look first at contemporary history in terms of its great achievements, the strong points of its total movement. What is there to be seen that confirms the biblical hypothesis about the present age?

The first thing is surely the very *awareness of history*

which has become such a fundamental and central piece of our mental equipment. Both in the universities and beyond, whatever we think of—the United Nations, or nuclear physics, the building industry or French literature—we think of it as growing from its last stage and growing towards the next. It is not a question of defining the stages of the immediate past and the immediate future, but of seeing everything referred to quite simply and inevitably in terms of evolution, growth, or development. We very often put a value on this. Terms such as 'development', 'new', 'old-fashioned' have taken on positive and negative connotations which in any strict sense they do not deserve at all. Why should a nation develop? Why should new techniques be better? There are voices which insist on these questions, and rightly so, but by and large this way of thinking has irrevocably entered our system.

A further point within it is that we see history not only as moving, but as accelerating. The rate of change is difficult to measure, but the impression is very widespread that in many ways, whether in scientific discovery, social upheaval, or educational needs, we are moving faster than our fathers did and must be prepared to see our children outpace us. Moreover, we can never know exactly where things are going. In any particular field we can see what developments have taken place and can make intelligent guesses and forecasts for the future. But the future, we know, will never be exactly as we imagine or plan. New insights, factors, and possibilities will arise and propel the whole in new directions. 'History has become systematically changeful in ways that are inherently unpredictable' (J. P. Corbett). Thus there is less and less in our world that is static and sure: all insights and institutions are becoming relative, both promisingly and threateningly open to the unknown future. Is this not strikingly congruent with what the New Testament has to say about the new age succeeding to the old?

Along with this goes the process of *the unification of our world.* This is most obviously seen in terms of the political and economic history of our times, when the decisions and actions of men in one part of the world are more and more affecting those in any other, and when the development of genuinely international institutions becomes a vital necessity for the very continuance, let alone improvement, of present conditions. But this unification is also to be seen in humbler fields, for example higher education. At one level here there is the amazing phenomenon of foreign students. At the moment large numbers of these come from the 'developing' to study in the 'developed' nations, but the phenomenon is becoming more and more general and the traffic increasingly diverse. At another level the international congresses of academics make clear that knowledge, most obviously in the natural sciences but in principle just as much in the humanities and social sciences, takes no account of nationality. No doubt the universities of each country aim to serve primarily their own society, but there is an internal logic in what they do that impels them at the same time to do what others do and develop common institutions by which it can be seen that their service must in principle be offered to the entire and single world. Cannot this unity be seen as a shadowy prefiguration of the promised unity and harmony of all things at the end, indeed as a step towards this?

Another very widespread development concerns *the place of man in the universe.* From being merely one species among other creatures and equally subject to the impersonal processes of evolution, men have long since risen to a position of power over the rest of nature, a power that will soon involve us in creating life and controlling the weather. We shall be less and less at the mercy of natural forces, but rather their master, and not only of those of terrestrial nature but of those of the whole cosmos. There can be little doubt that man is in the process of taking control of the created order and can shape all things, or distort them, more and more to his own liking. Along with this has gone a challenging of all that is held to be supernatural or super-human, to the point where the immensities of space, far from terrifying, can be seen as the wide open spaces of tomorrow, and where religion is most commonly explained as a human need or complex.

The corresponding features in the university lie perhaps in the inevitable disappearance of any élitist conception. The university is at the service of the whole of society, and all who are capable of it should benefit from it. No longer is it the case that the content and method of education are given and man required to measure up to it; rather must the contents and methods serve the true needs of man and continually be adapted accordingly. Of course there remain many complex questions within that adaptation, but the basic thesis is but rarely challenged, that what men want they must be able to have and that the rest of the universe is there to be used by and for men. Those who claim to know God, the ultimate, in terms of one particular man will see a particular meaning in this growing centrality of man.

Within all this our age is offering to each and every man *far greater possibilities of choice*. The university student, for example, can increasingly choose the subject he studies, the job he will do, and the wife he will marry, for himself. Fewer and fewer of our choices and decisions are inevitable or wholly determined for us by social traditions and con-ventions; where they are, students are among the first to rebel. But more than this, our age is increasingly forcing decisive choices on us. To this the permanent availability of nuclear weapons is an eloquent witness: it lies within the power of men to choose, and that at any moment, an action which could destroy the whole of what we mean by civiliza-tion. At another level, the striving for some democratic pattern of government, to which almost every nation at least pays lip-service, is a sign that the decisive choices are being distributed among the many and cannot be retained, at least not simply, by the few. At the same time as we are increasingly freed *from* external restraints we are increasingly faced by the challenge of what and whom our freedom is *for*. This can not only remind us of the radical freedom of Jesus himself, but also point to the nature of his authority. The choices he put before those who met him will now be increasingly, one can almost say inevitably, faced by all the rest of us too.

On none of these points so rawly mentioned can we expect to find neat patterns. All these aspects of our times are dynamic realities, all moving, changing, developing among myriads of people and situations which defy easy generalization. They all presuppose a tension between where we have got to and where we shall one day be, a tension that is already strikingly akin to the New Testament's historical outlook. But we should also see a congruity between our experience of ambiguity and complexity, and the New Testament message of the hidden Lordship of Christ. Our times will never simply and clearly point to their ruler until they are fulfilled. Until then there will always be much that argues against the claim that it is he who is in charge. For now just as in his life-time he never imposes on human freedom, the freedom both to accept or oppose his rule.

On the one hand, man's selfish use of his freedom will continue to thwart the purposes of Christ. Every new development inevitably opens up possibilities for good and evil at the same time. Ours is the century of Auschwitz, thalidomide, and senseless slaughter on the roads quite as much as of space technology and the eradication of malaria. On the other hand, man's noblest achievements are grounded in the discipline of freedom. The adventures of research and democracy, like those of art and love, require openness, dedication, and faith; any watertight certainty or prepackaged answer reduces them to dust. The best can only be had on the condition of risking the worst. One may say it is no accident that the beginnings of the age of affluence should coincide with the beginnings of the age of nuclear threat. And yet the very sustaining of the constant ambiguity can be seen as a mark of Christ's hidden but active rule.

Christians must always be careful in talking of history like this. Direct claims that 'God is at work in history' invite much misunderstanding and quite proper scorn. In the first place, we should not lay claim to be able to interpret the *whole* of contemporary history: we may believe that it is all in the charge of Christ, but all any of us can expect to see are signs which, given our faith (and it is faith, not sight), seem to fit in, to make sense. Students in the USA, for example, have been seeing sit-ins and protest marches as signs that Negro emancipation shares in the humanizing purpose of Christ, but it might in the end all turn out a bitter failure. Secondly, we must frankly say that it is because we entertain certain hypotheses about the man Jesus that we recognize any such things as signs of growth towards the fulfilment. This may on occasion agree, but is much more likely not to, with the interpretation the world at large draws from those same realities. Christian students in Germany, for instance, have seen the division of their country as the proper price to be paid for its responsibility for the world war, but that is hardly a popular opinion.

In the third place, the perceiving of signs is the function of the prophet, and while many of us are called to prophetic obedience, the New Testament suggests that the peculiar and perhaps isolated insights of the prophets need to be submitted to the whole Christian community for testing and ratification before they are fit for proclamation and use. This has happened most impressively in the way the Vatican Council has ratified previously isolated ideas; if only all the churches were able to do so with similar eagerness. Moreover, prophetic signs call for active response, not mere acknowledgement. An armchair prophet would be a contradiction in terms. A Korean who suggests a remedy for his country's ills and then flies off to North America hardly deserves to be taken seriously. To see some development in the modern world as a sign of Christ's active Lordship is to know oneself and the whole Christian community called into active participation in his purposes with it.

In further limitation it must be said that it will usually be much easier to find such signs in the big things of history, the epochal developments and main trends, about which we necessarily speak in approximations and generalities. The smaller the phenomenon, or the more precisely we know it, the more we will be aware of the confusing complexities, of the large scope of human freedom, of the difficulty of interpreting it at all directly in terms of the activity or purpose of Christ. Prophecy belongs more to the temper of the enthusiasts of the last chapter.

Nevertheless, it is one of the central strivings of the Christian life to try to lay hold of reality in these terms, to see the whole movement of our world, including that of human understanding, in this overall perspective. It is as any phenomenon, any happening, any situation can be interpreted within this total framework of history that Christian faith begins to know how to deal with it. When we see, for instance, the political independence of Africa, or the civil rights movement in the USA, or the choice of a subject to study, in terms of their place in the total movement of history from the resurrection to the fulfilment, then we can explore what our own obedience in relation to them is to be. Without this or some such vision, man becomes history's slave, not its author.

Some Trinitarian tidying up

When Christians are involved in this sort of discussion about history, the terms 'God', 'Christ', and 'Holy Spirit' tend to occur in somewhat disconcerting variety. Do they refer to anything precise? Here perhaps we should pause and attempt a little Trinitarian tidying up! The doctrine of the Trinity is probably one of the pieces of the Christian tradition least evident to us of the 1960s, and I would never want to claim that a full and correct understanding of its intricacies is essential for every Christian. For all that, however, we do need it in order to make sense of our experience, provided that we are careful to use its terms with some care.

Briefly, a meaningful interpretation will always start with the man Jesus, who in his life showed us both the purpose and destiny of our human history, and who beyond his death is active, if hidden, in bringing our whole history to its fulfilment. But he refused to see himself as the centre and origin: invariably he referred his own life and purpose to 'the father'. By this title and relationship he pointed to Yahweh, God as the Jews knew and worshipped him. But Yahweh, even for the Jews, was a hidden God, and since most of us are not Jewish Christians but Gentiles—who when they use the word 'God' refer only to one or other of the Baals—we need to be very careful not to ascribe to God activities and properties which Jesus would not have linked with his father. Our Gentile communication with God is only sure if it is through Jesus, through his relationship with his father. Even Jesus is now hidden to us, but before leaving the original disciples he handed on to them what they called the Holy Spirit.

At this point there is a lively debate going on nowadays. Some Christians, as they find signs in the world of its movement towards the promised fulfilment, interpret these as signs of the work of the Spirit. 'The Spirit,' they might say, 'is obviously active in the civil rights struggle in the USA, in the campaign against the present South African government, and so on. Therefore we must be, too.' Others find this dangerously enthusiastic: in every discussion some Germans will say that that sounds like the language of those Christians who supported Hitler. This second voice points out that in the New Testament the Spirit is always spoken of in relation to the church, never to secular events, and so seems to refuse any possibility of ascribing events in history to his leading.

But is there not a way through, faithful both to our experience and to the New Testament? In this the Spirit is undoubtedly what is handed on to the disciples so that they will truly *understand* who Jesus is and what he means, so that they will *remain in communication* with him and therefore with the father, so that they will *continue his work* of making available to all men his service and his understanding, and so that they will be infused with his personality and *live out his life*, no longer their own. Each aspect of this gift is baffling and offers dangerous possibilities for arrogance, so that one must always insist that it is in Jesus that the true nature of the Spirit can be seen: if we ascribe anything to the Spirit which we could not to him, we go wrong. But just as Jesus' whole efforts were directed out from himself to other people, and in principle to all men, so the gift of the Spirit to the church is not given so that the church may shut herself off and enjoy it, but precisely for the sake of the church's whole relationship to the world. At each point in that relationship it is the conscious understanding given in the Spirit—and which is not automatic or natural—that ensures that the church really does stand on the basis laid by Jesus and is not wandering after a passing fashion.

By ascribing personality to the Spirit, the early church pointed to the experience that the initiative was from him to them, that they were caught up by an outside force, not handed a tool to use as they like. In our day we probably seldom experience a direct handing on of the Spirit such as at Pentecost, but is it not still true of our deepest experiences that their movement is predominantly towards us and not under our control? You cannot choose to fall in love or make a scientific discovery: they happen to you, even if what you have or have not done previously will make a decisive difference. The most fundamental decisions of faith and commitment are made in the context of a com-

pulsion from outside, of a truth or an opportunity that it
would cost too much to deny. It is in connection with that
sort of experience, measured as always against the person of
Jesus, that one can justifiably refer to the Spirit.

The contemporary scene: the weak points

So far we have been thinking of the 'strong' points of history in terms of the Lordship of Christ, but there is another
and no less vital aspect of the New Testament experience
which is congruous with our contemporary history and experience: that the man in final charge is also the man who
was crucified. The majesty of Jesus is not of the triumphal,
bragging, and self-glorifying sort, but is at its most truly
majestic in humble, vulnerable, and self-forgetting identification and service to others. For this reason our vision of
history must also pay considerable attention to the 'weak'
points of history, the poverty and the suffering, the people
that are overlooked and forgotten. Here the reductionists
have their distinctive contribution. Jesus' availability, humility, and solidarity with the outcast were no mere tactical
characteristics of his life, put aside when he ascended. If he
is Lord today, he is still the serving, vulnerable, and cruci-
fiable Lord who expects no better mount than a donkey.
Moreover, he promised his church that if they would see
him they must look among the poor, the oppressed, and the
outcast: it is being with them and serving them that we
shall find and know him.

The realistic student will notice time and time again that
as Christians simply and unassumingly go to wherever there
is need and try to be of some help, they point more effectively to Jesus' Lordship than the best prepared of ecclesiastical political declarations. It may mean a team of doctors
devoting themselves for years to the cure and prevention of
leprosy in some isolated region; or a group of students seek-

ing out the lonely and the bewildered amid the hectic pressures of a commuter university and spending time on befriending and helping them; or others deciding to use their valuable and specialist skills in a 'backward' community where salary, housing, and promotion prospects are at best dim. They can suggest, and that with the authenticity of action over and above the necessarily theoretical commerce of words, that it is Jesus who is the dominant ruler and that the values seen in his life are the ultimately true values.

What can be seen at the 'weak' points of history is, paradoxically, far more the presence and power of evil than those of the man Jesus. But our obedience within them will help both us and others to discover of what sort and how real his sovereignty is. Our vision and interpretation will be based on his personality, his way of serving, his demonstration of human freedom. Sometimes in the affluent West it is difficult to spot obvious points of need. We shall not consider as outcast and suffering those whose chief lack is of a second television set! In our day the glaring unfreedom from ignorance, disease, poverty, and oppression of so much of the world remains a challenge to action; but if, as we may hope, the material needs of men are increasingly met in years to come, then it will require an increasingly sensitive, open, and discriminating eye to see where the real weak points are. At that stage the tension between different visions of human fullness may become crucial.

At the same time, this insistence on the weak points of history must also be qualified by a reminder that service of need loses its truth and value the moment it is controlled by some ulterior motive. Time spent on helping and befriending overseas students, for instance, is vitiated if they come to feel it was essentially devoted to making them Christians. Christians are to suffer out the inhumanities and frailties of history with no assumption of merit, of security, even of success in any direct way, and this is to share in the permanent co-suffering of Jesus which is also his majesty and triumph and which, we may believe, is actively bringing on the climax and fulfilment of history.

For suffering, both in the New Testament and contemporary experience, is a sign of the onward movement, even of the advance of history. It is often remarked that the twentieth century has provided both the greatest humanitarian achievements and the most appalling sufferings in history. And this is what is suggested by the New Testament teaching on the powers of evil—that they have been essentially defeated but are still working up to their greatest defiance and conflict with the power of Christ. Christians need not expect to have less of the sufferings of Christ to fill up as history moves towards its goal in him, nor to see in their lifetime the victory and the triumph. Their job is to be sensitive and available, expecting nothing for themselves but the faith, itself unprovable, that their service is in fact a reflection and a part of his.

As we look out then at this history of ours, and try to make sense of it and discuss its meaning with other people, we must look and talk about both the strong and the weak sides. Many will see no significant connection between them, but it is one of the distinctive features of the Christian vision that it sees both in the same framework of understanding and can integrate them. Here again, the enthusiasts and the reductionists both belong to and need one another.

Not that the church should expect any particular power or monopoly because of this comprehensive vision. Whether it is a case (on the strong side) of achieving a nuclear test ban treaty, discovering the biochemical formula of a living cell, surveying the route of a new motorway, or (on the weak side) of eradicating illiteracy, solving the problems of old-age pensioners, or helping the less gifted students to make something of their studies, Christians can at best offer a contribution within an effort shared by many and which needs no particular label. All of these things may happen without explicit Christian participation: in every case it is the world—not excluding its Christians—which draws up the agenda. What the church can do, and it alone, is to explore and offer a conscious interpretation of all that goes on in terms of the achievement of Christ and of his advancing purpose, and then to throw its own influence and weight into the effort to move history in Christ-ward directions.

Christ is the same and his purposes constant on both the strong and the weak sides of human life. His presence, whether as sovereign or as sacrifice, is implicit in both. More than this, the church's interpretation and appropriate participation make the weak into the criterion for the handling of the strong. The affluence of the western world, we must say and work out, is not simply to be enjoyed by the West, but is given for the sake of those who do not yet share it: nuclear disarmament should allow more adequate provision to be made for pensioners; the purpose of a motorway should not be to allow the rich of the industrial cities to speed every weekend to their seaside cottages, but to open up possibilities of transport and communication for the stagnant and depressed areas. Indeed, the church's own service at points of need can turn these into the strong points of the future. The salient example of this in our day is the ways in which the medical and educational pioneering of Christian missionaries in Africa and Asia has led, as the key initiative within a myriad of other factors, to the independence, growth, and power of the nations of those continents. Humble obedience in one generation may become a sign of victory two or three later.

A permanent danger in this kind of view of history, and one to which students are perhaps particularly prone, is that of building magnificent abstract visions which those actually living out the matter concerned will seldom recognize. Now, admittedly, there is always a need for the urgency and stark clarity of a prophetic insight to cut through the considerations of custom and comfort that determine far more of our lives than most of us can admit. And yet there will inevitably remain the stubborn complexity and ambiguity of worldly reality. In history we never know exactly what is right or wrong, we never reach the ideal. From our present stage of imperfection we can only pursue what seems to be better, and even that will turn out differently from what we thought and will offer room for improvement. Any enthusiastic vision must come to terms with the partial and provisional nature of human striving.

Jesus often told parables of growth. Between the sowing and the harvest, things are always unclear: other plants may be mixed in with the crop, the birds may eat the shoots, there may be a storm or drought. What man does or does not do in this period is certainly relevant and important, but what is decisive is the sowing and the harvesting. The metaphor is not an allegory that can be literally applied to the world's history, but it can encourage us to hold together the decisive certainties of believing and the relative ambiguities of living. Despite all the uncertainties and mysteries, we can know where we are headed.

For further reading

A study of the New Testament fundamental to this whole exploration of history is *Christ and Time* by Oscar Cullmann (SCM Press, London, and Westminster Press, Philadelphia). More directly useful for shaping our contemporary understanding is *Christ the Meaning of History* by Hendrik Berkhof, which has just appeared in English translation (John Knox Press, Richmond, Virginia, and SCM Press, London). *Christianity in World History* by A. Th. van Leeuwen (Edinburgh House Press, London), is a difficult—because complex and far-reaching—but extremely important attempt to discern the actual processes of the world's history in terms of the kind of framework I have sketched.

CHAPTER FOUR

The job to be done: Mission

SOONER or later in almost every student discussion of topics like these, someone will be heard saying, 'It is all very well what you say, but what does it mean in practice? What are we expected to do about it?' A vital question, and one not to be shrugged off as activism, for it arises from the insight characteristic of our times that the test of any idea lies in its application to reality. Students are properly impatient of any assertion whose relevance cannot be shown, and a student who calls himself a Christian but does not see that that involves him in doing something will not long remain one.

Unfortunately the word mission, which points to the doing which faith in Christ involves, is a typical piece of jargon—meaningless to all except the initiated. I find frequent occasion to recall the embarrassing evening when I gave a talk on it to a group of training college students, only to discover from their hesitant questions afterwards that the only meaning any of them could attach to it was that of a special week of meetings and services held some time earlier in a nearby parish church! It would be good to find a new word, but no one yet has. Meanwhile it is an indispensable word for any worldly Christianity; with what content can we fill it?

Fifty years ago mission was unhesitatingly equated with the foreign missions of the western churches; now it is generally agreed that by mission we refer to the entire task of the church, not only to some of the particular, let alone

unusual, projects in which this is carried out. It is a singular
word that can only be used for generalities and therefore in
the abstract, whereas what it refers to is a vast complex of
urgent, passionate, daring, even tragic things that are to be
done. Mission is not so much one entity as a whole way of
living—of feeling, of seeing, and of searching for love and
truth.

Similarly, it is misleading to talk of the mission of the
church as though we knew what the church was and could
deduce the meaning of mission from that. It is the other
way round: we can only tell what the church is in terms of
what it is there for. 'The church exists by mission as a fire
exists by burning' (E. Brunner). Christians discover the
church when they get down to mission. This chapter, in
reflecting a quest for mission, also reflects a quest for the
true nature of the church.

The job is his before it is ours

We have learnt to start, in mission as much as in everything
else, with the man Jesus. It is obvious, as a historical fact,
that if he had not lived, more particularly if he had not died
and come back in the way his followers asserted, they would
never have formed a church nor 'done' any mission. Their
mission, like the mission of each succeeding generation of
the church down to and beyond our own, depends upon
what he was and did. But this dependence—and here we
come to the central insight in recent discussions—is not only
a matter of past history, of the horizontal succession of the
church on earth from the man Jesus: what the church is to
be and do today equally depends on Jesus, now exalted, and
on what he is doing today in and with human history. That
is why the chapter on history had to come before this chapter on mission. We cannot carry the commission to the first
disciples directly over to ourselves; we have to see their place
in Jesus' total dealing with history, and then ours, which is

c

not the same. Jesus' call to us is not only transmitted from the first disciples: it also comes through our awareness of his total purpose and of our own position within that.

Some people then ask whether one cannot simply deduce the tasks to be done from one's analysis of contemporary history without bothering with the man Jesus. Of course you can if you want—most people do; but the chances are that you will very soon fall into the limited terms of a particular ideological view of history or of a determinism by which, in practice, you are merely seeking to impose your own will or your own understanding on others. If it is to be the Christian mission we undertake—i.e., the mission performed by Jesus during his lifetime and which he is still pursuing—then we must insist always on finding our obedience at the intersection of *two* kinds of awareness: awareness of the man Jesus and of his commands to the disciples; and awareness of the contemporary world under his rule and impulse. 'The Christian'—how often has this been said at student meetings—'holds his newspaper in one hand and his Bible in the other, and finds his obedience where they meet.'

What Christians are to do in the world is not merely up to them but depends on what Jesus has done and is doing. Mission is response to his mission. Several key points follow from this. The first runs directly counter to the individualism of our age. We almost automatically think of Christian faith and obedience in terms of the individual: again and again a sermon will reach its climax by appealing to an isolated 'you' as though but one person and not a dozen or two were sitting listening. Of course the individual is vitally involved and nothing can happen without his readiness and decision. But it is the wrong way round to start with the faith of the individual, to suppose that one part of his obedience involves the community of Christians to which he belongs (whether a parish congregation or a student group) and then that through that community he contributes to the life of the whole church and so to the purpose of the Lord. Quite pragmatically, as a matter of history, it was only because of the man Jesus that the church came into being, and only as the whole church grew that this and that local group was formed and this and that individual set on the way of faith and obedience. In the same way, theologically, what matters in the world is what Jesus has done and is doing. The appropriate missionary response is to be made by the whole church; within that response each particular grouping finds its opportunities and tasks, and within their comprehensive undertaking each individual his.

This is no excuse for any kind of church totalitarianism whereby mission is merely a matter of obeying orders from above. But it is the only framework in which we will grasp the universality of the Christian task and get over the debilitating distinction between the normal and the special in mission. The feeding of the hungry in India might be taken as the missionary obedience of a few 'foreign missionaries', yet if the conquest of hunger is one of Christ's chief purposes today, then that is the job of the whole church, and many more of us in all countries should be finding ways to take part in it. It will help us, too, to see the ways in which the witness of any individual is both conditioned and completed by that of the church as a whole. Behind a Hindu's asking for Christian baptism (or a Christian becoming a Buddhist) stands a whole host of factors and events, never alone the influence of a single conversation or a single relationship, even if the person concerned might point to some such as determinative.

Second, if mission is a response to what Jesus is doing with the world, then we must take seriously its historical conditioning. Its immediate purposes and forms will quite properly change and vary as the years pass and history moves on. The obvious example is again in 'foreign missions': a hundred years ago it was inevitable that missionaries should go almost entirely from Europe and America to Asia and Africa. Now that the countries and churches of

Asia and Africa have moved into independence and responsibility, there must be far more interdependence, and
in fifty years' time it may be appropriate for Asia and Africa
to be sending large numbers of Christians to pursue the
mission in Europe. History is always thrusting us out of the
old understanding and the old pattern; in each new situation we need to go further and search afresh for what our
obedience is to be now. To student committees I have often
found myself saying, 'If you do it simply because they did
it last year, then it's wrong!'

Third, if the Christian mission is above all a response to
Jesus, then nothing falls outside its concern. He is not only
concerned with any particular 'religious' or 'moral' field:
resurrection has happened and is promised of the *body*, not
of any 'soul'. Therefore the job of the church too has to do
with *all* things and not just with certain limited domains—
with big business and the transport system just as much as
with marriage and the education of children. Mission is not
one task among others; you cannot assign it to a particular
committee alongside others dealing with finance, pastoral
care, and worship, just as you cannot allot it a few hours a
week along with others devoted to recreation. It is a dimen-
sion of all we are and do.

For this reason mission is essentially the affair of the laity.
To appeal for 'the whole church to join in the struggle to
free the world from hunger' is not primarily to ask various
international Christian institutions to decide in their appropriate committees to collect funds, train farmers, and actually grow the food required. This may be part of what is
involved, but such an appeal is addressed to every Christian
and asks him to take up the struggle in whatever ways his
daily life offers. Farmers who are Christians should try to
grow more, bankers and industrialists should try so to order
their businesses that financial and commercial movements
favour and encourage international economic justice, and
all of us who have a vote should so take part in the discus-

sing and persuading of politics that governments break out of the habits of protecting national interests and try to act in a spirit of international philanthropy.

This is why there are many who insist that the church is not essentially opposed to the world. The New Testament often speaks as though it were, for by 'world' it means the 'fleshly' world of human self-interest. Yet most of us follow common contemporary parlance in meaning by 'world' the whole order of things, what the New Testament sometimes calls 'the earth', and of this the church is of course a part. Yet it is not just a part *of* the world; it is a part *for* the world. It aims to be representative of the world in the sense of 'acting on behalf of' the world, to seek nothing for itself which it does not also seek for the whole world, and to affirm nothing about itself which it does not in principle also affirm for the whole world.

This is, paradoxically, a 'particular' function. To hold to this all-inclusive purpose does in fact lead to a certain distinction from communities with different or only partial purposes. The church can never accept as its own the role of one 'religious' party among others or that of a club for those who happen to like what it offers, even if it is bound to appear as such in the eyes of many. For what gives the church its peculiar function is its relation to Jesus. He was, and is, the world's representative who acts on behalf of the whole world and who claims nothing for himself—not even the relationship of being 'Son of God'—which he does not intend and pursue also for the world as a whole.

Christians are all, as it were, knots in that vastly complicated web of relationships that make up our world. Within this pulsating web of human society there is the subsidiary web of Christians, seeking out the points where evil is flowing in order to accept, absorb, and nullify it in the strength and example of Jesus, and also making available in deed and word the peculiar knowledge about the web as a whole which is its gift and its task.

Response to the hidden Lord

In talking of mission as response to what Jesus is after we
dare not forget that the Lord of history is a hidden Lord.
We cannot know in detail the course of history but must
always act in faith, knowing both that we may be wrong
and, on the other hand, that forgiveness is always available
to empower a new start. This means that any particular
understanding or action of mission will always be relative,
partial, unfinished, and ambiguous. The certainty, the
wholeness, and the end belong to the Lord, not to us. Mission is always a sowing of seed: a lot will get lost and much
will have only superficial results, but Jesus has promised
that some will grow—secretly, you will not be able to see it
—and will bear an astonishing harvest. And this happens:
an argument in a student meeting may well influence a vital
political decision thirty years later, long after the man concerned has forgotten how he became convinced in that
direction. Yet even where we may suppose we see harvest,
this becomes as far as we are then concerned the occasion
and the instrument of further sowing: the missionary response to that particular political decision is not to sit back
and say, 'What a good Christian he is', but to look carefully
into what needs doing if that decision is now to have its
desired effect.

Mission cannot proceed more than one step at a time;
even if one probably needs an idea of the further possibilities
in order even to take one step, these should not be completely fixed but left open to see how the first one goes. If
you plan a series of discussions with Muslim students, it is
useless to draw up a list of topics 'the Muslim needs to
know about Christ'; far rather start by asking them about
Islam and see what happens from there—your own surprise
at things they emphasize or omit will be a far truer and
more effective witness than any predetermined list of points
to preach at them. This may look irresponsible, and so it is;

the responsibility is Christ's, and ours only in a derived sense. But it gives us a freedom and flexibility to respond in appropriate ways to the actual circumstances. These should be basic characteristics of all Christian obedience, but are extremely hard to achieve in opposition to a deep and universal human longing for security which leads us all to follow established patterns and to overlook the ways in which the situation might be changed.

Almost more important, the fact that in mission we try to respond to a hidden Lord should make Christians extremely chary about the kind of success to expect. What results from obedience, as far as formal and institutional categories go, is always secondary to the deeper changes that men cannot measure. I first became seized with this in visiting Pakistan. There Christians live as a tiny minority in a Muslim country, a minority often on the defensive and inevitably very self-aware. As a result it is all too easy to think of Christianity in communal terms, of faith as membership in that precarious community, and of mission as doing things that enhance its numbers or standing. This effectively paralyses any self-forgetful partnership with Muslims and any free and uncalculating offering of the good news of Christ.

In the West, too, are we not also good at labelling actions Christian or non-Christian as though something important was said by that? As our churches improve their machinery, not least under ecumenical pressures, so there is always more temptation to judge people by their stance in relation to that machinery, instead of leaving all such judgement to the Lord. We are in danger of falling prey to a new form of communalism and of forgetting that it is the hidden Lord and the world which matter, not our own inevitably fumbling efforts to be true to both.

There are times in history—say the Dark Ages in Europe —when the shifting circumstances provide an opportunity for Christians and the church to take the initiative in society with power and success. Yet there are also times when other worldly powers have the initiative, though always under the ultimate rule of the risen Jesus, and where the church's appropriate response to the opportunities it finds never leads it, institutionally speaking, into recognition or power (as it did not during the Dark Ages themselves). In many respects we live in a period of the latter type today. What matters is not the degree of visible power and influence, but the church's constant sensitivity to the opportunities thrown up in the movement of history. Its response to these may sometimes be bold and public, at other times hidden within situations of neglect and suffering; in either case it is striving to be the first-fruits of the new world which Jesus is bringing on. In this way there is an intimate interaction between church and world which, we may believe, is a finally determinative thread in the world's total history.

Mission in the university

As I warned at the outset, all this is inevitably schematic. The realities of mission are humanly complex and compelling beyond any neat description or planning. Let me try to bring it down to earth in terms of a university setting.

The first thing must always be to stress that Christians are to be *present* in the university. Just as Jesus was first and foremost a man among others, so are his followers to be. As indeed, of course, they are! It sounds nonsense to draw attention to such an obvious theme, and yet it would seem that by stressing the 'otherworldly' characteristics of Christian faith and hope the majority of churches have disposed their members away from seeing their involvement in various aspects of the world's life as entailing a conscious response to the work of Jesus. In our day, much of the struggle of Christian living and thinking is having to be devoted to the discovery of what it means to be a Christian, and therefore a missionary, within the processes of industry, broadcasting, suburbia, local politics, and everything else, including the university. And then what matters, before we ever come to any particular projects of service or witness, is the quality of that presence: not so much what Christians do, but what sort of people they are.

This quality has been called that of 'holy worldliness'. What is involved can perhaps be indicated by the use of the two words, 'awareness' and 'solidarity'. Christians are, first, those who are *aware* of the direction in which the world is eventually going, and of the man ultimately in charge. The great, universal assertions it makes about him are of course of a different order of awareness from that of the inner workings of a computer or of the recent political history of one's country. In these cases we are dealing with proximate questions, and here Christians have no short cut to solutions: they need to know the facts and to be guided by experience as much as anyone else. But they will be eager to be aware of the facts and to draw on the relevant experience, to be sensitive to what others are thinking and feeling, and to appreciate the deeper significance in any word or act. Their thirst for awareness covers the proximate as well as the ultimate questions.

Along with this awareness goes the related quality of *solidarity*. Just as Jesus was open and available to those around him, so Christians are to live at the service of their neighbours with a ready and active compassion for all that affects them. They, too, are to be vulnerable to the pressures of the world, to share an African student's rage and shame at being refused by the umpteenth landlady, to spend time helping an awkward pupil even if the exam scripts will then have to require some midnight oil. Both words point to permanently demanding qualities: the cross of unremitting study and of unwearied availability to others is indeed a daily business, even if a cross is not always the best image to describe it.

By this understanding of Christian presence a university

teacher who believes in Jesus is carrying on the Christian mission as he gives his lectures, takes his classes, marks exam papers, and delves into test tubes or manuscripts in search of new insights. In all these he is doing what his colleagues, Christians or not, are also doing, and in more or less the same way—in any case what he does and how he does it is probably more determined by his involvement with his colleagues than by his involvement with other Christians. The obvious question then arises: 'What difference does it make to be a Christian, and how can you talk of my carrying on the Christian mission if there isn't any?'

To this, one blunt voice tends to insist: 'There is no difference; your job is simply to get on with being a good teacher.' Another will counter: 'The differences are to be found in, for example, your reason for doing the job in the first place, as a service to others rather than as a path to prestige; or in your relationships with colleagues and students; or in the biases you have in teaching the subject matter and in selecting and judging research material; or in your conception of the university's role in society and the actions you undertake to pursue that.'

Both are right. The first is right in telling us not to spend time looking for differences between ourselves and others. Our job is simply to be faithful to what we have chosen to be faithful to. But the second is right to say that that is not enough of an answer. Yes, we are not to seek to be different for the sake of being different, but we should not be surprised if, as we are faithful to our understanding of what it means to be a good teacher, others notice certain differences and want to talk those out with us, or indeed to fight us. Moreover, those who talk of 'being a *good* teacher' must realize how many problems the word 'good' involves. A Christian will not be content simply to follow his own understanding of the goodness appropriate in his situation: he will actively want and need to pursue a discussion about it, both with those he might expect to agree with him, and with those he suspects would not. For in a university (or, of course, a trade union, a political party, a profession, shop, or home), however important it be that the community be open to people of all sorts of views, it is technically and humanly intolerable for them merely to follow their various understandings without a constant and lively discussion of what is appropriate and good in their situation—and that is precisely a discussion about the coming perfection or fulfilment where Christians, who see this in terms of the man Jesus, may find themselves saying and doing something 'different'. Yet all the time what matters is not that the Christians should be different, but that the university as a whole should play its part within the total activity of Christ and so help to bring the whole world to fulfilment.

On the basis of the given presence of Christians, the demands of mission are often conveniently divided into the two distinct realms of service and witness. Service primarily involves the 'feeling' side, the compassion and solidarity of Christians at the weak points of history, while witness takes up the 'seeing' side, the demands of knowledge and awareness in regard to the strong points. Yet, as we shall see, they always and inevitably involve one another.

Mission as service

Service is a popular theme these days, not least because it promises a radical break with all self-seeking and arrogance on the part of the church. Many students, and in this Christians are not too different, will respond to appeals for service where they would refuse any suggestion that they impose themselves on others. The exploration of service may well begin, as it seems to have done with Jesus, in quite individual terms: who is there among my neighbours who might need such service as I can offer? Looking around most universities today one can find the lonely, the bewildered, those with housing or financial difficulties, often perhaps foreign students, who can do with a bit of help. But as the example of housing immediately shows, service that would be effective will soon have to move beyond the individual plane to, say, the sphere of the student union or of the university authorities, by whom alone such needs can be properly tackled; direct, personal help is often not easy to give or receive, and yet it probably requires even more sensitivity, energy, and indeed organization to arrange for effective service at this other level. Further, it is often not enough, in the university conditions of today, to confine one's view to the needs of the university. If students are much better off, materially and in terms of prospects and status, than many others in the community at large, then service projects of yet another order may be called for in society. Students go out to collect money for refugees or to rehabilitate slum property. This in turn leads on: it is not enough to paint old people's houses if the old people have not enough of a pension to live off. Community service projects will often point the need for political action, no whit less genuine as service.

A rather different exploration, and in the long run a more important one, starts from the suggestion that service be the dominant motive in the very business of study. This will lead a student, in choosing between possible jobs, to choose the one by which he can best serve, and that in turn will influence his constant decisions about courses to follow and discipline and intensity in study. In recent years a number of Vocation Weeks have been held in universities, whereby a concentrated effort is made within a given week to face each student with the question of what job he will do and with the suggestion that his criterion should not be wealth or security or even interest, but service.

Many people, not least within the foreign missionary circles of the churches, have complained that this student interest in service represents an abandonment of Christian faith to mere humanitarianism. For of course it is possible to serve without being a Christian: one can be thankful for the fact without worrying about the label. At the same time, these critics overlook the committing character of service: as the example of Vocation Week shows, the question of his job is a much more real and challenging question, because it is one every student inevitably faces anyway, than the question of what he believes in. Indeed his choice of job shows what he believes in, shows it not least to himself.

Service leads on to the exposing of commitments in witness: if a group from a training college spend all their leisure hours teaching immigrant children in the slums, or if a reasonably able law student asks the Appointments Board to suggest a job for him in which he can really serve people's deepest needs and not spend his time on the affluent wastes of litigation, that already witnesses to the people around. It suggests unusual priorities, and at least implicitly raises the question to the observer why he is not doing the same. Service also inevitably leads towards witness as it succeeds in creating a new situation. Serve people in a slum by providing better houses and they soon start asking for better schools; help people to win freedom from material need and they approach the point where lack of true knowledge about the purpose and destiny of the world will become their immediate need, a need which then can only be served by witness. People sometimes reproach the Christian ideal of service with turning those who follow it into no more than a doormat on which others can wipe off their troubles. Yet because service entails witness in the long run, that doormat (to extend the metaphor in a somewhat ludicrous direction) is also one of those vibrant machines which, when you step on to it, shakes up and revivifies your whole system.

Mission as witness

While service is unassuming, witness is concerned with the explicit stating and sharing of belief. It has become an un-

popular term among students because, mixing daily with
others from Asia and Africa, they see all too clearly the
misuse which Christians have made of western power in
those countries in the name of Christian witness. Respect
for the other demands a respect for his convictions. But it is
a false step to move from there to the supposition that witnessing is invariably arrogant. The word has become a piece
of technical Christian jargon, whereas it points to a quite
normal human activity. We tend to think of witness as
happening in a situation where a Christian is speaking to a
non-Christian about Christianity, but that is only one of a
myriad of possible situations. A couple coming out of the
theatre witness to one another about the play they have
seen; politicians witness across their platform about the
paths to be followed; the professor witnesses to his students
about the significance he sees in a certain experiment, and
they to him as they write their exams. These may or may
not be Christians; the process is the same. For witness is
nothing more than the attempt to share with others those
things (experiences, ideas, possibilities) a man feels to be
important. Since the Christian feels the man Jesus to be,
overall, the most important thing he knows, the most important relationship he stands in, he will certainly want to
bring into that sharing a pointing to Jesus, an offering of
the meaning he finds there. But not at every moment; only
when it comes up naturally; and not in laboured discon-
tinuity with the rest of the conversation.

Moreover, the activity 'witness' has become disastrously
confused with the result 'conversion'. To witness is not to
cajole or argue other people into accepting your point of
view or joining your community: it is to do no more than
point to what you believe to be significant and true, or to
offer a criterion and an interpretation in which you find
meaning or purpose. You point and you offer in the company of another person; there is no sense in doing so by
yourself. But the response the other makes is his business,

his free decision. He may ask you, as a theoretical question, what the consequences of the offer you make are; he may as part of his acceptance ask you to suggest what he should do. But the responsibility for the acceptance is his and the consequences of the acceptance are his; you cannot assume the one and cannot determine the other. Witness is the affair of the Christian; response to that witness is the affair of the other; conversion is the affair of the Spirit.

The peculiar interest of Christians in any dialogue in which they are involved will be to push through to the deeper questions. Not every time, of course: to insist on facing a neighbour who wants to know whether a geography lecture is at ten or eleven with the question why he studies geography anyway shows less awareness than a lack of proportion. But in fact hidden in every proximate question and answer are more ultimate considerations. The middle, the place where you simply get on with your experiments without bothering about extraneous and deeper questions, is always bounded by the horizon composed of these (terms I owe to Professor C. A. van Peursen). The dialogue of witness leads on to these in such a way that the basic options are exposed and new decisions become possible.

Witness, then, is an everyday procedure, and witness to Jesus can start from and be implicit in every possible exchange, as western travellers in the great non-Christian civilizations have often realized with astonishment. This means that the witnesser actively needs his partner in dialogue, not simply as someone to talk to but as the person from whom alone he can receive the occasion and form of witness. The world, here as always, writes the agenda. If a historian who is a Christian finds himself in conversation with, say, a biologist or any other specialist in a particular field not his own, he as a Christian is going to have to listen very hard indeed and is going to have to put many questions from his side in order simply to discern the points at which some relation can be seen between the rule of Jesus Christ and biological knowledge, and before he can really begin to offer some possibilities of significance and purpose.

There is a yet deeper level to the mutuality involved in witness, namely that the impact and significance of the man Jesus will come alive, often in quite new ways, not only to the one addressed, but also to the one trying to disclose them. To stick to the example of the biologist: as he explains, say, the limitations of biological study methods or the nature of the data which support the hypothesis of natural selection, the listening Christian, trying to hold what he hears in relation to the rule of Jesus (let alone to his own specialist training and experience), may himself see a meaning and importance in certain aspects of the life of Jesus or certain traditional ideas about him which he would never have realized outside that conversation. The exchange of witness is never one-sided. Indeed, 'One only really learns the gospel in the effort to communicate it to others' (Lesslie Newbigin).

An open community

Both witness and service, while inevitably to a large extent initiated by Christians, are at their most authentic when they happen as response to a need or an idea thrown up in the world. Both are more concerned with the other person, and with the hidden Christ implicit in that other, than with their own adequacy or correctness. The direction of Christian vision is always away from ourselves.

This may be part of the reason why an awareness of what mission really means is now leading to an often impassioned debate about the 'openness' of the Christian community. We seem to have inherited the model of a congregation or group of Christians all of whom are quite definite about their Christian faith and commitment and who meet to discuss a certain problem or plan some piece of action on that accepted basis. Yet this model is seldom borne out in reality.

When a meeting is called, say, on 'Man is no better than a computer', or when there is an action being launched to help overseas students, to take only rather obvious examples, then the Christians involved will very likely find themselves agreeing with and working with others who would not call themselves Christians. Indeed, the whole point of the activity is to involve those others. But what then happens to the accepted basis of the community? It seems to become more like a general debating or welfare society, and someone will soon be complaining that this is to dissolve the church into the world, to abandon Christ's call to the decision of faith, and to lose hold of that tradition by which alone any community can justly be known as Christian.

To see the way through this problem will certainly take some time; it is vital that we hold on to the worldliness we have gained and not slip back into relying on a refurbished but still exclusive mentality. Clear theological thinking is called for, and some points are already emerging. Most people agree that it is the world as a whole which is the object of Christ's purpose, not just the church, and therefore that it is entirely right that Christians should be concerned with the whole life of the university (industry, nation, etc.), and not only with some special category of 'religious affairs'. They are Christ's instrument in the university, and should be in contact with and yoked with anybody and everybody else in order to build up and improve not their own community but the university as a whole.

Yet one may ask why debates about the nature of man or projects of service to overseas students should be specifically identified with the Christian community; perhaps there are times when this is the only conceivable way to get them done, but most universities have developed more appropriate machinery—the student union, say, or a welfare committee. In that case the important thing for Christians is to see that *those* are open for the expression of all points of view and for the co-operation of every willing hand, and not

limited in fact or in principle by some ideological consideration. The Christian mission, pursued in the world, requires
and furthers an open society.

What then are the particular activities of the Christian
community, if mission takes place in the union and the
coffee bar, not primarily in the chaplaincy? Surely, its particular, limited task is to provide what is needed in order to
ensure that at least some of the opinions expressed in the
debate, some of the motives to service, and some of the
vision by which either are arranged are based on knowledge
of the ruling Jesus. The function of the Christian community is that of providing for those whose search has led
them to him, and who are trying to live by him, a place
where they can explicitly talk over and work out together
questions that face them. These activities will, of course, be
open to any who want to come, to those also who are not
quite sure whether their search is leading to him, as to those
who simply want to see what's going, but it will be clear
what the basic purpose of the activity is, and that it does not
take place for its own sake but for the sake of the wider life
of the university.

In other words, the basic thrust of openness is from
Christ into the whole university—and that in turn into
society—not from the whole university into the Christian
community. The church, it has been well said, is a 'go-
structure', not a 'come-structure'. Of course one cannot go
from nowhere: a certain 'come-movement' will always also
happen, as Christians—and others, if they want to—bring
questions they have met in the university into a common
exploration of understanding, attitude, and solution which
deliberately includes Jesus Christ as one of its data. Christians are to know one another and to share together in a
community whose centre is acknowledged to be Jesus Christ,
but this is always and in every way towards and for the sake
of the wider community, in principle the whole world, whose
centre is equally Jesus Christ, usually unacknowledged.

The view of mission which seems to be emerging, and of which I have only indicated the theoretical structure, may seem to many to be very activist and optimistic. 'Here is the world on its way to fulfilment in Christ; we only have to join in and help it onwards.' Is this more than the ever-repeated but ever-misguided optimism of another younger generation? Time alone will tell, but I hope so. I hope so, first, because this basic optimism of faith nevertheless takes account of and expects the many manifestations of men making choices away from the fulfilment in Christ; the Christian mission certainly includes witnessing against false witness and serving in spite of opposition and scorn. But also because in this view it is not what we do that really counts, but what Christ is doing: our active response can help, but our uncertainties and failings cannot finally hinder his aim. Precisely since we are so aware of our own uncertainties and failings in face of so universal and overwhelming a promise-demand, there will always be one *leitmotiv* of mission which looks away from activism and says, 'Thy will be done'. Our more strenuous obedience in mission should never hinder our quieter obedience in its counterpart and complement, worship.

For further reading

In the nature of the case more is to be found in periodicals than in full-scale books. Two very useful books written for study groups are *Where in the World*, and *What in the World* by Colin Williams (National Council of Churches, New York, and Epworth Press, London). An outstanding example in practice of this kind of mission is movingly told in *Come out the Wilderness* by Bruce Kenrick (Harper and Row, New York, and Fontana/Collins, London).

CHAPTER FIVE

The other job to be done: Worship

WHATEVER can a worldly Christianity make of worship?
Is this not precisely the point at which full weight must be
given to the 'other-worldliness' involved in Christian faith?
Christians who are drawn into taking more and more seriously the realities and demands of their experience of the
world are often to be found criticizing most of the worship
they know for being at best irrelevant and at worst a process
of deliberate self-deception. And yet the church continues
to insist on the centrality of worship, both in practice by
retaining it as its main, often its only activity of the week,
and in theory by rounding off innumerable discussions, sermons, and statements, even the most practical, with an
'After all is said and done, what really matters is that we lift
our hearts to God . . .'. (I hope that this chapter will at
least avoid the sanctimonious tone of voice often associated
with such phrases!)

Is it possible to be fair to both the contemporary frustration and the traditional insistence, to struggle towards an
understanding and practice of worship which is fully open
to the contemporary world *and* which continues to see
worship as central to human living?

Personally, I believe so, but I must be aware, in saying
that, of the very tentative and fragmentary nature of the
contemporary discussions towards it. Not that there is any
lack of discussion about worship itself: the universal church
has by now built up such a rich and enthralling tradition of
worship—if you see it that way—that those who are inter-

ested can find an unending exploration in its varieties and developments. But very seldom does that discussion bear on the relationship between worship and what is happening in the world at large, or even on the relationship between worship and mission.

For me, what has come to be the central, liberating, and fertile insight is this: that worship and mission are directly parallel and complementary terms. The church exists by participating in the reality of the world, on the one hand, and of the risen Jesus on the other (through him, some would say, in that of the Trinity, but I need not go into that here). Just as mission is the content and expression of its participation in the world, in the name of Jesus, so is worship the content and expression of its participation in Jesus, in the world's name. In mission the church turns her concentration and energies upon the world; in worship they are turned to Jesus. More crudely, as mission is what the church does in the world, so worship is what the world does in the church. Worship thus comes to be just as comprehensive and complex a term as mission.

Worship, too, is primarily his job

Worship is what the church does towards and in relation to Jesus, and through him to the father to whom he always referred. It is the traffic of the relationship made available in Jesus and which has become for Christians the relationship which is deeper than and which conditions all others. To look at it this way can perhaps help us beyond a frequent argument. Preachers and theologians, at least those who speak English, since there is no equivalent word in many other languages, are fond of saying that worship is 'giving worth to something', or 'the acknowledgement of whatever comes first'. To this the sceptical student is likely to reply, 'How can I say what comes first? At different times I am dealing with different things and so follow different levels and priorities.' True enough: that is inevitable in as complex a world as ours. The fallacy is to introduce the word 'things' when it is a case of personal relationships. These, too, may change, but at any particular time each of us can give some answer to the question, 'Who is for you the most important person?', even if it must often in honesty be 'myself'! The traffic of such a relationship, whether with oneself, with a husband or wife, with father or mother, with one's boss or with the leader of a party is, if it goes deep enough, worship. The Old Testament may have been right after all to insist that the fundamental alternative in life is not between being 'religious' and 'secular', but between worshipping him who is worth worship, God, and worshipping those who are not, so making them idols.

To see what may be meant in a worldly understanding of worship, we shall have to cover again much of the ground involved in the discussion of mission. Here, too, we have to start not from any supposedly universal human need for God, nor from any categorical command to worship—neither of which cut much ice with students—but simply from the original experience of that man Jesus. His disciples found that for him it was a constant and perfectly natural aspect of life to be referring himself and other people to his father and to be holding the situations he was involved in to that father, whether by going off by himself for a deliberate time of prayer, or within the business of his everyday contacts. That relationship to his father was clearly crucial for him, and he gave time and energy to upholding it. It was his own particular relationship; even if as a Jew he talked of it in terms that he found in his people's scriptures, he lived it more intimately and radically even than the great figures of the Old Testament. But he did not hug it to himself: he was continually telling others, particularly the disciples, about it; and if his return to them, after his death, was aimed at one action above all others, this was, as they saw it, that of handing on to them his 'spirit', that of making available to them that intimate and radical relationship which had been the basis of all he was and did. They, the first disciples, were good Jews and continued for a time to observe the Jewish practices of worship, but the distinctive acts of worship—the breaking of bread, the baptizing of new disciples—these came from Jesus and took place because of him.

There began the tradition which Christians today inherit. But the historical Jesus of the reductionists needs again to be completed with the active Lord of the enthusiasts. It is not just his past relationship which Christians today can take up in worship; it is his *present* relationship with the father into which they are taken up by the mysterious but promised Spirit. When thinking of mission we rightly concentrate on his contemporary activity as ruler, but in terms of worship we should remember that he is also the pleader: he is not only the source of the father's manward activity; he is also the source and bearer of man's activity towards the father. To say that Christian worship is fundamentally our response to and participation in his worship may sound like no more than one of those metaphysical stock phrases which anyone brought up in the Christian tradition cannot help unloading now and then, but in fact it is meant to be taken quite realistically. Here, as at other points, the practice and explanation of worship by Christians may go beyond what others want to do and say, but it is not for that any less pragmatic and 'worldly'.

This basic point helps with two of the most familiar difficulties about worship met in student circles. The one has to do with the painful limitations we are aware of in our own worship—let alone other people's. The language we use may be stiff, the hymns we sing uncongenial to our experience, the whole pattern and shape apparently inadequate for even the stammers of love we should like to try to put into it. This is, of course, no excuse for not trying to improve things, yet even when we do try we realize the shaming limitations and inadequacy of what we arrive at. The same is true in mission: even when we bring every imaginable resource to play on a particular political or social situation, this can remain unhealed and unwholesome. In either case we can take heart for the continuing struggle from the realization that what matters, in the long run, is not what we do or leave undone—though this matters in the short run and we are certainly not to do less than our utmost—but what Jesus has done and is doing. Any sort of adequacy or success, in worship as in mission, is to be found in him, not in us, and is his business, not ours. We can be free to do our best and not worry about results.

This already overlaps with the second problem, that of the effect of prayer. 'What difference does it make to pray?' 'What do you think you are actually doing in prayer?' are questions which come up over and over again. The second deserves a perfectly honest and empirical answer: 'I am taking a certain amount of time to concentrate on Jesus and because of him on the father, and then to concentrate in that setting on people and situations I am in contact with; I simply hold the two together in my mind, if necessary quite inarticulately. My own feelings and desires about those people and situations may of course be involved, but it is not they which matter: it is my holding of the world and some of its parts into what I know of Jesus.' As for results, the most visible ones are those that involve the person or community praying, the new attitude or action which may result from spending five minutes on such a juxtaposition. They can well be results enough. But it is also possible to believe, since it is above all Jesus' pleading and his energies, however hidden to us, that are involved, that our bare five minutes and inadequate concentration are contributing in some small but genuine way, just as we trust our fumbling acts of service can do, to the bringing of all things towards that fullness of their inherent potential and of relationship with the father that has been foreshadowed in the resurrection of Jesus.

The word 'worship', just like 'mission', has been narrowed in use. We name 'University Mission' a special week arranged every three years or so, and 'worship' that which takes an hour of some people's Sunday mornings, whereas in fact they are inherent all the time. Both worship and mission are 'dimensions' of all we are and do. The whole of living can be seen and lived as worship, and that not because every choice and act is accompanied by a momentary 'arrow' prayer, but simply because one cannot step out of relation to Jesus. (One can step out of consciousness of it, and for that reason arrow prayers may be useful, but many of us find them unnecessarily cluttering.) This relationship, together with the relation with the world, can be made a permanent criterion for the assigning of priorities and for the pursuit of depth in living, and so a permanent tool of self-criticism. To take some other criterion, or to follow no steady one at all, is equally to make use of our human responsibility to determine where each choice and action stand on the spectrum that runs from self-centredness to self-sacrifice, but worship and mission, of one sort or another, will always inevitably be happening.

At the same time, the direction of our concentration differs: at one moment we shall be concentrating, whether mind or will, on something of the world; at other, and probably rarer moments, we shall be concentrating mind and will on Jesus. Therefore it is right *also* to talk of particular acts and occasions as (acts of) worship and mission, but only as a precipitation and focus of what is always already inherent in living.

The more 'radical' of Christian students can today be heard saying, 'The purpose of Jesus has to do with the university, with what goes on in lectures and the committee sessions in the student union, and it's there that I meet him, there that I do my worshipping.' Certainly so, in the fundamental sense of the word: it is in an authentic struggling into the future, with others and with the whole of the situations that face us, that we acknowledge in action the priority and worth of Jesus. Such a declaration needs no correction; yet it can do with a supplement—that because it all is indeed a struggle, in those lectures and in those committee sessions, we need to think from time to time what we are doing it for and into which future we are trying to bring them.

The world in worship

The church's practice and discussion of worship have come to seem off-puttingly introverted and unreal to many acute students. This is precisely the opposite of what ought to be, for in its acts of worship—and here again we take up one of the insights arising out of recent discussion of mission— the church is acting as representative of the world, is a part of the world acting on behalf of the whole. Each individual or group of Christians, whether in their overall worship of studying, voting, and raising their families, or in the acts by which they focus this, is in intention offering up to and through Christ the whole of the world as they are involved in it and thus allowing him to hold the whole to the father. Worship is not, we are realizing, something that happens between the church and its head—the world being as it were momentarily shut out—but something that happens between the world and its head, the church being the instrument by means of which it can happen. Or again, we tend to think of acts of worship as times when God or his son is especially close to us, when he comes and makes himself known to us. This may all be true, bar the especially, but only as a consequence of the more basic reality and purpose of worship, that here the world is consciously offered to him. The movement of worship—do not our hymns and prayers betray us?—is Godward; the manward aspects and results of worship are secondary. For God is as close to us in a vote on the common agricultural policies of the European community or in a sick neighbour as he is in our prayers, and makes himself known there to those who have eyes to see. What we do in acts of worship is to recall, consciously, and in the light of the occasion when he was fully present and known, his contemporary presence and activity in the world, and to offer it all back to him.

For this reason it is up to the church to see that it is indeed the world which is offered up in worship. Many recent discussions have pointed to the danger that a too free use of the word 'God' may in fact lead us to worship someone else than him who is known to us as the father of Jesus. We need to be at least as aware of the danger—in many contemporary churches an imminent one—that our worship involves not the stubborn, complex, and precarious world in which we in fact live, but only a relatively simple and even comfortable world made up of a few private feelings and family relationships. Since the church is a typical part of the world in most respects, it should feel free to offer up in worship its 'own' world and not always somebody else's, yet the real effort and struggle of worship is precisely that of involving the *whole* of reality in the action of Jesus.

Almost all churches know this in terms of intercession, where we pray not only for ourselves, not only for Christians, but first of all for the world and what is happening in it, for political tensions and struggles, for economic justice and development, for all who are sick and suffering. . . . But do we in our thanksgiving offer thanks merely for those things for which we happen to feel thankful, or for all those things for which the peoples of the world are thankful? Do we in our confessions of sin remember and turn from things we ourselves happen to have done wrong, or from those things we know in the world and read of in our newspapers which are evidence of the estrangement of mankind? (If we think of the H-bomb or the number of deaths on the roads at

Christmas time, then indeed 'the burden of them is intolerable'.) Do we in our adoration offer up the praise we find in Christian hymnbooks or can dredge out of our own undernourished emotions, or do we delightedly offer the technological accomplishments, the political treaties, the academic theses, and the all-out rhythm in which the world most typically and genuinely expresses its appreciation of what it is and what it has in it to become? It is not surprising that in many student circles intercession is the only form of prayer which retains meaning and validity. The recovery of these others will often burst the bounds of the prayer-form as we have known it. Adoration might come to require gathering around a computer or playing over the spokesman's announcement of a general ban on nuclear testing. Confession of sin might be most truly evoked by the haunting pessimism of a nihilist poet or need to come to grips with an academic disdain for the implications of society's demands on the university.

It is well known that public worship has again and again become alive and appropriate at times of crisis or triumph, at times when the realities of the world force concern, confession, or joy upon us. Cannot it be the task of the church's worship, a friend once put it in correspondence, to be just as urgently concerned *all the time* about what is going on around it? Is not worship the result and sign of a serene yet serious struggle with the reality confronting men in order that our awareness of this may help to bring it into the fulfilled rule of Jesus? Is not the drama of the common meal our human playing over of the drama of history, with all its changing complexity and variety, so that it is shaped into the drama of Jesus and his people? This is certainly an 'enthusiastic' way of looking at worship which will always need tying down to the actual man Jesus the disciples knew, and to the actual world we today live in, but it is, I suspect, a crucial pointer to the renewal of public worship.

If so, we shall need to look not, as many student groups

have tended, to a simplification of traditional liturgies, necessary as this may be for the sake of honesty, but to a wholesale transformation of their elements in terms of the world of today in the name of its ruler and representative. The element of formal and stylized cult in Christian worship is entirely appropriate so long as it is composed and maintained in a human awareness of what is happening in the world; it becomes damaging and dangerous when it serves to balk that awareness. We need poets to write the liturgies of our times, those who can give the rest of us words to express and offer with appropriate urgency our common and typical experience; perhaps, indeed, we already have them if we but knew where to look.

Here we come across another constant theme of recent discussions and one which I have already discussed in terms of mission. Christians today need to know the laity as the bearers and performers of worship, over against all habits and tendencies to make it the domain of the clergy. It is the laity, we have seen, who live and work scattered throughout the many sectors of the world and who can there discover, in terms of each particular situation, the service and the witness which the ruling Christ makes available to them; so also they can there discover the appropriate worship of that sector and situation and make it available to the awareness and public worship of the church as a whole. The function of the clergy is at best to preside over, co-ordinate, or express the symphony of worship whose melodies and harmonies come through the worldly experience of the laity. It is intolerable, for instance, for a sermon to be preached as it were *at* the laity from a platform of insight which they do not share (as distinct from a lecture offered to them from the particular and specialist experience of one of their number), where it should be a reminder, indeed a celebration, of the place of their own experience within the history and work of Christ with his world.

Three levels

The traditions of the churches suggest three different levels of focal acts of worship: private prayer, corporate services, and the sacrament of Holy Communion. I should have listed them in the reverse order. For when thinking of worship, as I mentioned in discussing mission, we tend to start from the individual and his own prayers, and then to see those contributing in some way to the worship of the congregation, which in turn feeds into the worship of the whole church, as though each congregation were basically a collection of individuals and the church a collection of congregations. Now of course there are occasions when it is appropriate to see things that way, but it is on the whole more true, not only to historical fact, let alone theological theory, but also to our personal experience, to start from the other end. It is the pleading of the risen Christ which enables and situates the worship of the universal church, the worship of the church as a whole which gives rise to the worship of each group within it, and the worship of the community which empowers and supports the private prayers of its members.

Let me try to illustrate this. Private prayer, i.e., the thoughts and words by which a Christian explicitly remembers his relationship to Jesus and reaffirms the intention of what he is spending his time on, is often these days a lost cause among students. Partly it is a case of the model becoming too rigid. We need to see that prayer can be as much the semi-articulate thoughts of a teacher on his way into the classroom, or of a doctor coming away from a sick-bed, as a regular daily period in which we can look over and hold to the father all that the day will involve or has involved. Partly it is a matter of the rhythms and pressures of the kind of life we lead today just not allowing for the originally monastic disciplines suggested by all the little books on how to pray. Still more is it a case of prayer having become meaningless because it is isolated: to be 'alone with God' for five or fifty minutes seems to cut us off from any meaningful context. But to share those minutes with a group, or even only one other person, so that the conversation with the risen Christ is also a conversation between human beings, provides a deliberate and purposeful context for explicit concentration on one's profound beliefs and intentions. Our prayer is not then 'our own', but a function of the offering of the group. If we spend most of our lives among and in relation to other people, it is appropriate that the focus of that life should also be in community.

The second level is that of those acts of common worship by which a particular group of Christians together reaffirm and remember their common loyalty and intention. These will be of every possible form and frequency, from, say, the daily prayers for ten minutes at lunchtime of those in down-town offices, to a special service held all over the country every five years on the occasion of the assembly of a new parliament. Diversity is obviously important here; different ways of being involved in the world require different forms of worship. And it is the knowledge that the worship of each group belongs to and is supported by the worship of the whole church which provides the vital freedom for Christians in different areas and settings to explore different forms and habits in worship. If we were each responsible for the genuineness of our own worship, we should have to hold to certain standard and external components to ensure that we have not lost contact with the universal. But if it is rather the worship of the whole church which carries and enables that of each community of Christians, whether in Hindu India, Marxist China, or a pluralist university, then certainly each can experiment with what might be characteristic of and appropriate to their own particular setting. To see our own worship as participating in that of the whole church frees us to be ourselves and not more than ourselves, one diverse part in a unity greater than we can know. The world always writes the agenda, and no value-judgement need be involved in comparing various forms, provided they all genuinely reflect an imaginative and sensitive grasp of the worldly situation.

At a third level there is the worship of the universal church in the meal which Jesus ate with his disciples before and after his death. This is, in the first place, a way of remembering Jesus and what he went through in the last week of his life. But then, particularly since the disciples after his death found him most often reappearing to them during a meal, the way of remembering who he was and what he did became also the way of remembering who he is and what he is doing now; to recall his acceptance and endurance of what men did to him became to recall the communication with the father which he has ever since been making available. In this way the continually repeated representation of his death and resurrection has rightly become at the same time the representation of what is really happening in and with the world, a dramatic celebration of the working out of what was then accomplished.

But it is not our action. What we do only represents and reflects what is being done by the risen Christ. (Some Christian traditions would want to talk here of the 'worship of heaven', which sounds dangerously unworldly; if so, translate it into terms of the whole Christ, the-head-and-his-body —it is not meant to posit some quite different category of beings.) This point again saves us from relying on ourselves, from the burden of needing to apply any kind of criterion of success or achievement. The church is simply to offer up the world as fully and honestly as it knows how, and need not worry about the final effect or value of its acts. That is his business. It also frees us to be aware of the worship offered by the world outside our ecclesiastical contexts. St Paul in Athens discovered the Greeks worshipping an unknown God, and offered to tell them about the person to whom they were in fact addressing themselves; it is up to Christians, in each different age and situation, to do the same by offering a direction and, where necessary, consciousness to that relationship with Christ in which each and every part of the world is in fact involved. It is not up to us to manufacture worship from nothing; we rather join in that which he is already offering to the father.

The search for new forms

The universalism of Christian worship should therefore not in the least involve Christians in throning over the world in splendid but, in the end, irrelevant separation. They are to be, and are, right in the thick of it, discovering and to some extent inventing the forms of worship by which the world is held through the risen Christ to the father. This quest of forms is very often the place at which students stumble upon a rediscovery of worship. It may involve, say in Japan or Nigeria, an exploration of possible ways in which worship offered through Jesus can take up ceremonies and songs deeply rooted in the culture of a people but which originally had a reference to some other ruler and which have first to be emptied in order to be refilled with new meaning.

In a modern university it may involve a long-drawn-out struggle to see the relation of criminal law, aerodynamic engineering, or zoological classifications to the purpose of the ruling Christ and to give expression to that in a form which a community of Christians can offer. In either case— as in that of all the other vital efforts of adaptation and indigenization—the results of the exploration will involve not only an acceptance of the surrounding world but its transfiguration, even conversion, by its being consciously turned into reference to the intention of Jesus for its own final fulfilment. Criminal law made available to the total purpose of Jesus can no longer be a business of applying an arbitrary assortment of legislation, or of abstract standards of right and wrong, but must understand the processes of the disease and healing of the relationships within a whole

D

community; zoological classifications no longer exist merely as items to be stored away in memory, but are an instrument by which human history can embrace the history of nature and so bring men and animals into a single community.

These random examples already show that, within the quest for more adequate forms of worship, the understanding of what is happening in worship is even more important than the precise form. A new form, unexplained and not understood, is almost useless; similarly, a full and historical understanding of the most traditional forms will often show them capable of carrying more worldly meaning than they seem to at first sight. In either case the form of worship can never be taken for granted: it will need some teaching and discussion about it even if these can already in part happen by its very use.

Moreover, in an age in which words, by too frequent and wrong use, can so easily lose their value (if perhaps less in the university than in some other settings), recent experiments are showing that what is *said* in worship is on the whole subordinate to what is *done*. The sacraments in which, however residually, the actions of a meal or a bath are the basic form retain their attraction and meaning far longer than services made up of words alone; a discussion or dialogue in which people can be seen to be sharing, and sharing open questions, is often far more readily accepted than a sermon which seems only to be peddling prefabricated and inapplicable pronouncements. Many go further still and find in active service of their fellow men an obedience and authenticity they have never even glimpsed in public worship. The world, of course, needs words, the tools of consciousness, as well as actions if it is to reach a fully personal fulfilment, but a stress on the actions involved in worship, and on its words as part of an action, will often help us in the search for more adequate forms.

In the church today we are gradually recognizing that

people in different cultures will not only need different languages, but also different actions and to some extent different understandings if they are really to offer in worship the world as they are involved in it. But we have hardly begun to recognize how much diversity this aim should also involve within a single situation, say that of a university. Private prayer, to start again at this end, will mean one thing for a student of art or literature who spends his days trying to comprehend and analyse the depths of other men's awareness of human relationships, something else to a science student constantly occupied with the regularities and interconnections of matter, something else again to students of history and political science whose view is directed to interpretations of men's corporate purposes in the world. These each have a rather different struggle to see what Christ is doing with the world as seen in their studies; so, too, they will have rather different forms and contents in their worship. Similarly, weekly services—if the week still offers an appropriate frequency—for first-year students will be one thing; those for university teachers will need to be considerably different; and those which bring the two together something else yet.

This diversity must also affect the celebration of the common meal, though here, since it is the same meal that is shared down all the centuries and in every grouping, there must be a careful balance between the single action of universal scope and the various particular circumstances in which it will be offered. A frequent celebration, say once a week, by the Christians in a particular faculty or residence may be quite a simple affair, while a celebration once a term or year in the context of the whole university will appropriately be much more formal and elaborate and will demand correspondingly greater preparation. In either case the basic character of the meal should be apparent: we should not just be present but actively prepare it, eat it in the company of family and friends, and clear up after it.

The common meal in the university

How can it be made to reflect the life of the university? The traditional model of the celebration has three parts. In the first part, the community gathers; many will know one another already; for others introductions will be necessary. They exchange news: news of what each has been involved in in his faculty, the books they have been studying, the experiments undertaken, the plans in hand for the coming period; or it may be news of the students and staff one lives with, or of the university union and the political and sports clubs. Gradually there is brought together an awareness of the whole university, and hopefully not just an awareness of the externals but of the real personal relationships and happenings that make up its community.

The second part is then occupied by an explicit dwelling on the man Jesus: who he was and is, and what he means for the university. This might take up Bible study done in groups or by individuals in the previous days or weeks; it may be led by some biblical expert or by a few of the laity who have deliberately prepared it. In any case, it will work towards a common understanding of the man and of his purposes as they affect the future, and it will probably lead to certain decisions, corporate or individual, about things to be seen to in the coming days or weeks. It will end in a corporate affirmation by all of their conscious relationship to Jesus, and thus to the entire church, an affirmation which by seeing the world in terms of him reminds them again that their missionary obedience is always part of his.

The third is the meal itself, which by taking up both those earlier stages becomes, in a most concentrated form, the drama of the university's participation in the total history of the world. The basic framework of eating together is not just incidental—after all, the fact of a common meal, whether a university banquet or a family dinner, does remain a potent sign and instrument of community even in our individualistic world. First, as it were, the table is laid; the community concentrates its awareness of the university into prayers of adoration, confession, and intercession, and offers the whole university through these into the pleading of Christ. Then, taking up their knowledge of him recalled and deepened by their Bible study, they give thanks: for all in the university and the world that in spite of human limitations is worth giving thanks for, and beyond that for the life of Jesus, for the relationship with the father made available in his resurrection and for the promise of final fulfilment.

In the breaking of bread and the act of sharing, there is presented, demanded, and accepted the radical openness of Jesus to those around him, his availability to others, and his refusal to put his own desires before their needs; and so an equal openness and self-sacrificing availability of the Christians present, not only to one another but to the whole university. Finally, the community disperses into all its various occupations throughout the university in order to live out and work out there the drama of Jesus' purposeful rule and men's reactions to it which they have played over together in archetypical form.

The celebration of the common meal arises in the first place from the missionary obedience of Christians in the worldly realities of the university, and it issues in the end into renewed mission. The celebration is never intended only for the people actually involved. It is for them as the world's representatives; it is for the whole world through them. In the light of this, incidentally, the words of *The Book of Common Prayer* at the administration of communion seem precisely wrong: 'The body and blood given for *thee*'—no, for the world, through the church, through thee . . . '*preserve* thy body and soul *unto everlasting life*' —no, catch thee up into a lifelong and active struggle to realize the perfection of all things which Christ is bringing on.

In the end, therefore, it is not enough to see worship and mission as parallel and equivalent tasks. They actively involve one another. The church's representation of the world in worship, and its identification there with the suffering and death of Jesus, are only genuine if they are equally real in its missionary obedience. Just as it is hypocritical for Christians to pray for aspects of the world's life without being involved in the attempt to help those same aspects on towards their fulfilment, so it is hypocritical for Christians to offer confession for the evil coursing through the network of the world if they are not available to receive and dissolve it themselves. Prayer always has implications and consequences in mission.

At the same time, worship is a complement, in some circumstances a corrective to mission. For mission is necessarily a demanding and complex involvement in one or other part of the world, and in our kind of world today often a difficult and precarious business, where it is indeed hard to know what one ought to be doing. If we had nothing but the call to mission, it would be very easy to become either more and more bewildered, or more and more fanatical, in either case to end up by serving the power of this world rather than the rule of Christ. It is worship, not minimizing the complexities and limitations of mission but interweaving with them, which recalls that Christ's action is always prior and fundamental to ours and in the end more important. It is worship which insists on the accomplishment of his purposes in the resurrection and on his present sovereignty. It is therefore worship which enables in his people a freedom and a joy despite the ambiguities of the world.

In the present state of much in the church, that sort of argument can easily turn into the worst sort of otherworldliness: 'Things are so difficult during the week, but we have a happy time in church on Sunday.' This is fatal. Worship belongs with mission, but must never be seen as a filling-station, where a Christian's resources are charged in preparation for being progressively emptied in the world. Against that, it must be insisted that Christ in fact meets us as much in the world as in the community of the church, and that mission will certainly involve a discovering of who he is, and a charging of our resources in him, perhaps without our being aware of it. Worship is not something over against mission; it is the other focus in the ellipse of Christian obedience, and in that sense an inherent condition of missionary action.

Yet the full truth lies even deeper. Just as our missionary struggling with reality is our true worship, our proper Godward response, so our worship is already in itself an element of mission. For one thing, the offering of worship on behalf of the world is our quite particular service, mysterious perhaps even to us, but which we believe to be a vital service, and one, unlike most of the others, which no one but those who believe in Christ can make. Moreover, the urgency of prayer, the quality of community, and the depth of dedication will intrinsically proclaim the love and universality of Christ: we should not be afraid to open the doors and celebrate worship in the eyes of all the world. Jesus' embracing of his followers by the common meal into humble and dedicated service within *his* purpose is bound to face all present with the question of their deepest commitment and purpose. It was a student group in Indonesia, with a large proportion of Muslim members, who found that by putting the Holy Communion at the centre of their programme they were confronting those Muslims, and themselves as Christians, with a constant challenge to conversion and obedience that could be seen to be the challenge of the living Christ and no mere proselytizing propaganda of the church.

For further reading

It is distressing how little of the abundant literature on worship sees it in this sort of relation to the world. The outstanding exception known to me is *Liturgy Coming to Life* by J. A. T. Robinson (Mowbray, London, and Westminster Press, Philadelphia), which is also written out of a university experience. *The Liturgical Movement and the Local Church* by A. Shands (SCM Press, London, and Morehouse-Barlow, New York), is a good deal less 'worldly', but also useful, and there is some splendid provocation in *Only One Way Left* by George Macleod (Iona Community). *For the Life of the World* by A. Schmemann (NSCF, 475 Riverside Drive, New York) is a commentary on the Orthodox liturgy which goes surprisingly far in this direction. Since this book went to press I have been able to see *Worship and Mission* by J. G. Davies (SCM Press, London, and Association Press, New York). Here at last is a book which provides a biblical and theological foundation for worship in Christ that is truly concerned with the world.

CHAPTER SIX

Into the way of it: Educating Christians

'YOU may well be on to something,' say some voices, usually from an older generation, 'when you suggest that Christians should lay stress on the worldliness of their faith. But you must remember that in dealing with students you are dealing with young people who are inevitably immature and who need proper instruction and preparation. They cannot simply be launched into what you have been talking about. They must be carefully trained first.'

Stop and ask yourself how you react to that, and you will find yourself beginning to take sides in the last of the contemporary debates I should like to explore in this book. It is a debate about the nature and methods of Christian education. Many people simply equate Christian education with Sunday schools for children, and suppose that its subject matter is infantile and of no relevance to adult life—a shallow opinion in the light of the meteoric rise of the Sunday schools in the last century and their enduring hold in every continent. Others are aware of the possibilities of adult programmes of Christian education—those of the evangelical academies in Germany being among the most often quoted—but envisage these more on an *ad hoc* basis than in terms of a general strategy. What is to be provided for students: glorified Sunday schools or embryonic academies? What is really involved in the education of Christians?

The two contrasting poles of the controversy are these. On the one hand there are the people who start from certain given elements of Christian faith and life which need to be taught to each new generation: the creeds, the doctrines, the meaning of worship, the use of the Bible, certain ethical standards, and so forth. The learners must be drawn into a committed fellowship willing to pursue a course of Bible study, lectures, and worship which will prepare them for going out and applying what they have learned in the rest of their life. In a word, the dominant concept is that of nurture, the dominant image that of the knapsack which the Christian must carefully pack before he sets out on the journey of faith.

On the other hand, there are those who reject all that smacks of preconceived answers in favour of an acute sensitivity to the demands and opportunities of each new situation. They too value fellowship, but the fellowship of those they meet in that situation and who will join in responding to it, not of those who are already committed to one identifiable approach or solution. What matters is the teasing out and acting together, not any more general direction or allegiance. The dominant concept here is involvement, and the dominant image that of manna, the rations provided afresh each day for the people who advance through the desert without maps.

As always, neither view proves tenable at its starkest extreme. The second, for instance, is impossibly vague. One cannot proceed in life by sensitivity alone: there must be some sense of ideal or direction. Merely being sensitive to both sides in an academic dispute will not often help to resolve it. What guarantee can there be of anything objective, let alone lastingly true, in the choices made? But the first is not much better. Doctrines or ethical standards, for instance, mean precisely nothing in the abstract; one believes or follows them because they seem more adequate than other alternatives—i.e., in reference to the contemporary situation. Have not Christians for far too long presumed that what is true and right could be abstractly known and taught, or that the Christian fellowship was *a priori* worth joining? Alone the proportion of baptized Christians who as adults reject conventional Christian teaching, and that too in virtually every continent these days, should force us to reconsider. The second extreme has at least the virtue of avoiding all paternalism, a cardinal virtue for students of both the ex-colonial and the ex-colonializing countries. It will not satisfy just as I have stated it, but it deserves to be taken seriously in any attempt to penetrate beyond the entrenched opposition of the two.

Lessons from general education

Any such exploration must of course take account of the analogous discussions and strivings in the general realm of education. The very term, for instance, is still commonly held to refer to a process directed towards a point where education will cease in favour of that which it was education for. A child is sent to school, and later on to college and university, in view of the moment when education has fully prepared him for adult life and he is released into a professional, social, and family career. For the rest of his life he is to use and give out what education has put into him. By no means only in the jibe, 'Those who can, do; those who can't, teach', does our common parlance suppose a distinction between teaching and doing, between learning and applying. Christian education has been assimilated to the same pattern; Sunday school finishes with admission into full church membership—and the proportion of those who are no longer effective members a year or two later is probably much the same as that of school leavers who breathe a sigh of relief that they are now out in the 'real' world.

Yet for university students that whole pattern is unreal. We learn in order to equip ourselves for more learning: *teaching leads not only to doing, but also to profiting from doing.* Moreover, in almost every field from the rarefied to the humdrum—even cooking, in an age where foreign pro-

duce becomes widely available—human knowledge increases
and moves on so fast that all sorts of continuing education
and re-education become necessary. Learning and doing are
not two consecutive stages so much as two constantly related
elements, and the term 'education' refers to the whole. Once
you really embark on the process of education you are
involved in it for life.

This affects the content: teaching methods in almost
every field are laying more and more emphasis on learning
from experience and on avoiding merely theoretical book-
work. Physics and chemistry have for long been taught in
the laboratory; in our day, modern language courses reject
the grammars in favour of tape-recordings and the so-called
'direct' method; nature study is done out in the field instead
of from wall-charts, and even history masters take their
classes to the local public records office or involve them in a
nearby excavation of Roman remains. *Experience precedes
and enables the interpreting and ordering of it in education.*
We live not by a simple deductive pattern of learning and
then applying, but by the more complex and adequate inductive pattern: experience, then the formulation of a
hypothesis which must be tested in new experience and
duly reformulated . . . in other words, by a continually
interrelated process of doing and learning.

Another misleading assumption is that the object of
education is the isolated individual, whereas it becomes
increasingly clear that education deals with the individual
within and for the sake of the community. Education trans-
mits the accumulated heritage of the community so that
the new generation can use and develop this further in
interchange among themselves. *Education is always initiation into a community and a tradition.* It is for this reason
inevitable that western education, the product of social
traditions in the West, should when introduced into Africa
occasion considerable tensions; indeed, it still does in Europe
and North America now that some parts of society are being

newly introduced to the full range of educational opportunity. In previous ages the initiation has often been into a static tradition, and education a neutral, even conservative influence in a stable society, but in our time an education with a predominantly inductive pattern is a critical and revolutionary force that inevitably contributes to an unknown but certainly changing future.

The priority of experience

These few remarks, however elementary, point to much of importance for the education of Christians. I have suggested that Christians are those who base their lives on the faith that Christ rules, hidden but active, over human history, and on the vocation to participate in his dynamic purposes there. Does that not go strikingly well with an insistence on the priority not of theory but of experience? Nothing occurs outside history; nothing is therefore insignificant or irrelevant to the purposes of Christ. Experience does not have to be identifiably 'religious' to contribute to the education of Christians. Every experience can be educative if you make it so—including, of course, the experience of thinking or the experience of realizing that *not* doing something is more appropriate and valuable than doing it: in insisting on the primacy of experience, I do not intend to commend any naïve activism. For experience leads to the asking of one's own questions, and so to a quest for adequate hypotheses and to a rigorous testing of those available. Any resulting assurance will be personal, honest, and real, and open to a continuing search for meaning, a constant re-testing of insight and commitment.

The faith that the whole of history is in the hands of Christ frees us from any particular starting-point in Christian education—whether Galilee, the love of parents, or what happened in church on Sunday. Since any experience belongs with the totality of history, one can start by exploring the significance of virtually anything: food, sex, or politics, studies or sports, confident that that exploration, honestly pursued, can lead on to the fullness of meaning in Christ. To give a group of students an introduction to Christianity, it will probably be far more effective to arrange for them to spend some time in a situation of urgency or crisis than to give them a course of lectures, however full and correct. Rather a profound insight into one genuine experience than a theoretical acquaintance with however many of the classic Christian verities.

At the same time it is Christ, we believe, who rules in history. That means, in this connection, that the exploration of the full significance of any given experience must involve the testing of the hypothesis available in the tradition of the church. No one can know that it is Christ who rules who has not encountered the memory of the man who lived in Palestine. At first sight this is no more than one hypothesis among many; history might be better explained by means of the memories about Lucretius, Krishna, or Marx available in the traditions of other communities. None of them is any good until it has been tested against experience. It is only in the situation where a man has learned to ask his own questions and to test various hypotheses that the Christian memory has a chance to be heard, weighed, and accepted.

Experience and memory: newspaper and Bible: each requires the other. Experience without memory is like a babe in arms: full of life and potential, but completely helpless. The Bible without the newspaper is inert: what it offers can only be true and meaningful as it becomes so for particular people in particular circumstances, whether an Ethiopian chamberlain on his way home from Jerusalem, or a Ghanaian student on his way home from medical studies in Russia. At one student conference recently the period of Bible study was directly followed by the reading of the headlines of the day's news, and in ten days there was hardly one where a vivid relationship could not be felt. Even if such immediate juxtaposition is not always possible, the study of the one should always have the other in mind. The two not only belong together: they each spur us on in the continuing struggle for meaning and obedience. Further exploration of the memory commits to new experience; the dilemmas posed by the newspaper send one back to further study of the Bible. It is the provision for this continuing and deepening interaction that constitutes Christian education.

The enterprise of theology, the restless expression of the meaning of the man Jesus, must therefore be essentially the business of the laity. We have locked it behind dog collars in the pulpit, whereas it can only thrive in normal working dress and on the city street. The raw materials the theologian needs are the experiences of the politician, the trader, the doctor, and the market analyst, as well as those of the carpenter and the tent-maker. In fact, the theologian is not one among those others, but is each of them as he explores and expresses the significance of his own experience in the light of the biblical hypothesis; experience being inevitably personal, no one else can do a man's exploring and expressing for him. Certainly we need technical, academic specialists—the linguists, archaeologists, critics, and philosophers —to be continually extending and refreshing our knowledge of the biblical records; certainly, too, we need those who can reflect in a general way on the theological explorations of the laymen of our time in order to interpret and evaluate their place in the total tradition of the church. But the actual, living, and significant theology is done and made by those who live the world's life from within and who there wrestle to test out in action the hypothesis of Christ. This is the theology by which the world can find the word to express itself. Christian education is not the handing out of right answers, but the putting of people into situations which compel them to realize and give the right answers, the answers that have been realized anew in many situations down two thousand years of history, and which each age, even each man, will give in his own way.

One understands, then, that the central discipline in Christian education is church history, the awareness of this interaction of word and world down the centuries by which one's own contemporary activity can be interpreted and fertilized. A sympathetic understanding of why each generation acted out and expressed its faith in the way it did is the best possible aid to the search for obedience in our new age. The Bible must be taught, above all, as a history book; as a book that records and interprets a certain stretch of history in order to suggest a hypothesis about the whole; as a book of a bewildering variety of parts, each of which arose in a fresh response to a fresh historical situation within the whole; and as a book among many others which all deserve study and testing for their capacity to illuminate experience today, a book with no inherently special rights but which, some people find, proves more valuable and enduring than any other. Bible study should never start by taking anything in it for granted, should never fear the most radical or hostile of questions: it is often the posing of these that will help people break out of 'religious' assumptions and see the significance of the real, worldly suggestions the Bible can offer. Such an approach can integrate Bible and newspaper, provide a full and positive place for fearless biblical criticism, and yet insist on wrestling with the single wholeness of the biblical argument and on the 'integration of all one's reading about society and politics with that argument' (D. Baly).

The lay character of theology means, too, that Christian education in the university must be seen as having to do with the university's regular business, and not as a merely optional recreation, like gliding or golf. This is not to specify anything about the institutional framework: there are a number of most significant experiments going on in which theological education, often along with that of other 'religious' traditions, is integrated into the regular university curriculum, but still in most cases conditions compel any formal programmes to take place after teaching hours or even outside university buildings. In either case, informal, even casual discussions will play a large part, for it is vital that the experience explored and interpreted should include the daily experiences involved in being a student. We live in a single world, not two different worlds of the university and of the church, nor yet those of the university and society outside. In the available time, concentration will be directed now here, to physics, sociology, anatomy, or Serbo-Croat; now there, to student grants, Abraham, Brecht, or baptism, but all for the sake of the single whole. Just as the sociologist who finds meaning in Christ must pursue and test that within his explorations of sociology, so the Christian who finds meaning in sociology must pursue and test that within his explorations of Christ. No wonder the Student Christian Movement is known for meetings on 'Christianity and ——' (science, politics, sex, films, or anything else meaningful for students). These are no evangelistic trick to lure the student scientist or politician into swallowing something else, but a normal and appropriate wrestling with the wholeness of experience and of meaning.

Education in community

So much for the point that education starts from experience. The communal nature of education is also a point of vital interest for Christians. No one can learn much merely by himself. Just as he needs a family to grow up in, so he needs to live with other people, not least those he reacts against, in order to become himself. One can only learn to be a Christian in the company of those who make the hypothesis of Christ available for testing and of those among whom the testing is done. Now the necessary community should not be restricted to the community of the church. The Christian student should not be expected to start as the member of some Christian association from which he may later sally forth into the dangerous battlefield of the university. It works the other way round: those who live in the university community may want to be engaged in the community of those who seek to find meaning and to make a contribution to university life—say the student union; within that they may move in the community of those testing particular central hypotheses—the SCM, the Communist society, the Pan-African Union, and so on—and within those may align themselves with those committed to a particular faith or tradition. All four levels coinhere: it is not a case of transferring chronologically from one into the next. The Christian student will normally distribute his allegiance within all four, and it is all four with which Christian education has to deal.

To stress the communal nature of education is to say that it is not concerned only with the individual as an isolated unit. University education these days necessarily involves intense specialization. So does Christian education, since it is concerned with the particular gifts of the spirit in each individual. Yet in both cases we must insist that a man's individual knowledge and gifts only find their full, personal meaning and use as functions of the wider community. The European universities are taking up computer technology since their nations need computer programmers, while African universities are going in for agriculture in a big way since that is a prime need of their peoples. So Christian education must be busy raising up those who can see the place of automation in the history of salvation, and those who will be able to work out the social and ethical implications of new agricultural methods. Of course, the interest and aptitude of the individual play a vital role: we are not after a totalitarianism which forces people to serve the needs of the community as these are interpreted by a certain group. But the community, in the first place those immediately around a person, should have a certain say; it ought for instance to be possible for a group of students discussing their future jobs in the light of the man Jesus to suggest to one another the kind of job they think they ought or ought not to be looking for.

Moreover, the community we are concerned with is no mere miscellany of individuals: the quality and depth of their relationships are cardinal. It used to be a commonplace of the academic tradition that to bring students together with one another, better still with a man or woman who had advanced further along the path of understanding, was far more educative than their cramming however many facts. This ideal tends perhaps to wane under the pressures of technological specialization—though it comes back in the higher reaches there too—but it remains entirely valid for Christian education.

A speaker who has done or seen something authentic or real, however odd his views or stumbling his speech, is worth more than any merely fluent and correct lecture. A conference where students can meet those who have had to commit themselves in a risky situation is worth more than dozens of sermons from their own chaplain; his function is rather to help them make the most of that speaker or that conference, to help them keep on asking their own questions and to suggest where possible hypotheses may be found.

This already points to the further insight that the particular awareness and commitment with which Christian education is concerned are essentially corporate. Education into Christian faith must be education into certain convictions about the nature of true human community: this is no mere context or consequence. Jesus could not have 'educated' the twelve one by one: what they learnt they could only learn by living together and with him. Christian education happens in community, it results in community and it commits to community.

A last point arising from the educational insights I have

mentioned is that we need to overcome in Christian education, as the universities are beginning to, the debilitating
idea that education stops at the transition to adult life. SCM
programmes, it is often said, should concentrate on training: if Christians want to have a joint discussion with
humanists or Hindus, let them wait until they are sure of
their own faith. This cannot do. It ignores the fact that SCM
members are already meeting them, day in, day out, in
classroom and café, let alone in Christian meetings to which
they come out of interest. And it smacks of a condescending
paternalism, whereas both physically and psychologically
most students know themselves to be adults and rightly
refuse any paternalist imposition. But most important, in
effect: time and time again it is the experience of discussing
with humanists and Hindus that will persuade Christians of
the value of their faith, awaken them to its deeper and wider
implications, and send them back to serious study of the
Bible and the big books on Christianity and other faiths. To
pursue the dialogue of witness with those who think other-
wise, or to commit ourselves to service of those with other
needs, will inevitably involve one's own Christian education,
and theirs. In the university—and in most other settings, I
suspect—to educate oneself by asking questions of others
and testing their hypotheses with them is to engage in service and in witness in the name of the hidden Christ. In a
word, *Christian education is not primarily a separate and
different activity from mission or worship, but is one perspective by which to consider and direct the whole of a community's living obedience.*

Education and tradition

In all this, I have been trying to do justice to the protagon-
ists of the second approach, those who lay the stress on
worldly involvement and therefore on total flexibility of
thought and structure. Yet can they really cope with the

fact that education is always initiation into a *tradition*? Is it not often those students most involved in the student union or political societies who are the most critical of the traditions of the churches, and whom the churches soon cease to regard as Christians? Worldly Christianity and tradition hardly seem to go together.

Not so. That is a damagingly superficial view. Recent work on the topic (cf. the Faith and Order World Conference of 1963) is teaching us to distinguish between the *Tradition* of the church, the faith in Jesus Christ which moved the original disciples and was passed on by them down the generations, and the *traditions* of the churches, the many different habits and practices by which the many different generations and communities of Christians have given expression to their faith. To draw a precise line between the two is often still a matter of controversy between the confessions, but it is clear at least that such things as the biblical record, the ceremonies of washing and the common meal, the commitment of a man's will to Jesus Christ and his purposes—these belong to the Tradition and are to be shared in by all Christians; while any particular interpretation of the Bible, any particular form of ceremony at the common meal, any particular understanding of what the purpose of Jesus Christ requires of his disciples—these are more likely to belong to one or other of the available traditions. The traditions depend on the Tradition: they are of no value if they are not related to it, and their value is always secondary to that of the Tradition as a whole. On the other hand, the Tradition is not available except through the various traditions. To claim to find it in total separation from the presently existing churches is either to find something else or else to set up a new variant tradition of your own.

The mistake lies in seeing either as a fixed entity whose function is only to remain as it is. Both are more truly understood as moving, historical realities acting in functional relation to the changing circumstances of each new age. Certainly the Tradition stems from the particular and long past events of the life of Jesus, and is nothing if it is not the remembering and representation of those. Yet because the man remembered is claimed to be living and ruling also now, long after his death, the Tradition is not as it were an inert parcel of facts stored in the cellars of successive generations, but an active realization, in each new generation, of what the man who then lived means also for us today. It is like a fire, lit at one moment in time, but which goes on burning: it cannot but spread and change in quality as it comes to new fuel, but it remains recognizably the same fire.

Each new generation is to make as full and adequate a response as possible to the challenge of its own times and circumstances. The traditions will therefore quite naturally vary, though not primarily for the sake of rejecting the heritage of the past: we are what we are because our fathers, in their day and in their way, gave expression to the same Tradition. All the same, in a generally conservative setting that response may well feel crabbed and suffocated by the dominance of what was thought and done yesterday. Christian education is always initiation into a moving tradition, into the next stage of the tradition. Woe betide the educator who thinks he knows what the response of his fellow learners ought to be!

Christian education, therefore, like mission, like worship, necessarily requires the gift of critical discernment. Here again there is a close affinity with the proper work of a modern university. Because Christians are centrally concerned with the living Tradition of Jesus Christ, they will be radically critical of all the traditions into which it has settled, and set a high premium on the renewal of the church. Because they are centrally concerned with obedient participation in his work, they will be radically critical of each other's doings and will set a high premium on diversity and experiment in the Christian community. This may lead the impetuous among them, for instance the students, to despise and scorn the more staid undertakings of, for example, their parents, but there is no inevitable reason why the fire of criticism cannot burn with the warmth of love.

A last facet of the debate about Christian education has to do with the fact that it takes place in the setting of a fragmented church. We would stand in the Tradition as Christians, but are caught in the traditions and are Methodists, Roman Catholics, Pentecostalists, Greek Orthodox, and three hundred and umpteen others. Where do you start to relate the two? In the student scene this is a quite practical argument. Some say: young people must first be trained in the fellowship and tradition of their own denominations, and will then be ready to join in working with other Christians. Others say: what unites us is more important than what divides; let us join together and work out our differences in a single community. The former often have the advantage of numbers: particularly in western countries more students will come to activities that bear the familiar denominational label than will risk losing identity in a simply Christian structure. But must we not learn to say that the structures of education, Christian or general, need to be shaped in order to enable participation in history rather than to preserve the tradition? It is the task to which the ruling Christ, through the challenge of the worldly situation, is calling us that must give content and structure to Christian education and thus carry further the Tradition. It is as we work together on this or that with the others ready to do so that we discover we are Baptists, Anglicans, or Armenians by realizing the particular limitations and abilities we each inherit from our different traditions; at the same time we will there—and only there—see how much the common task both needs all our diverse contributions and calls us beyond them. Many of us in international work camps and conferences could echo the remark a senior student from the Berlin SCM made to me at the Strasbourg conference: 'For the first time I am realizing that I am a

German and a Lutheran'. The argument from numbers may mean no more than that students, like any others, will often enough welcome the chance to stay as they are and to avoid the challenging experience that could force on maturity. How it is in the primary school I cannot say, but at least in the university the deep end is a better educator than the steps.

The logic of the ecumenical movement

It is no accident that in the end this discussion on education and indeed the whole book should run up against the question of unity. For all the thinking I have drawn on has arisen in an ecumenical community, and it is the conviction of many that a stress on the worldly character of Christianity corresponds to the stage to which the inherent logic of the whole ecumenical movement has now brought us. From the beginning, the ecumenical movement has known itself to be a missionary movement: it has grown from a concentration on the obedience of Christians in the world. Yet this emphasis has moved and changed, so that looking back now one can see three distinct stages.

In the early days, say at the turn of the century, the focus was on the *gospel*, the good news which the individual Christian was to take out into the world. Christ stood behind and sent his troops out forward. Denominational traditions hardly mattered, since this urgent commission could be heard through them all. In the World Student Christian Federation, John R. Mott could involve Asians and Europeans, Baptists and Orthodox, in the same movement, almost regardless of the historical gulfs. Later, say between the wars, the focus turned to the *church*, the Christian community which was to spread the kingdom throughout the world. Christ stood now in the centre and radiated his influence outward on all sides. Denominational traditions needed to be carefully explored, compared, and reconciled so that the circle might be recognizably the same. The WSCF discovered the problem of intercommunion, and laid many of the foundations for the World Council of Churches. In our day, say in the 1960s, the focus has shifted again, to the *world*, that secular and universal community which is moving through history towards its fulfilment in Christ. Christ stands out ahead, incognito within each developing situation, calling those who can recognize him to follow up the opportunities he has opened. In the WSCF students throw themselves into social and political revolutions, the struggle for economic justice and for the adaptation of the university to serve the needs of society, finding in these the solidarity and the human urgency they see in Christ. Denominational traditions are at best the memory of earlier obedience: while they will inevitably shape our diverse contributions, they are to be transformed beyond their separations in favour of the larger perspective now available.

The model is rough and brief. It will not everywhere be true. But the student Christian movements are everywhere exploring into its many implications and discovering an authenticity and an integrity in Christian faith which on the whole our generation no longer expects from the churches. Will the way of a worldly Christianity prove in a century's time to have restored it? That, of course, is much easier said than done: the experiments and discussions are far from finished, and will never be so this side of the New City. To take part in them can admittedly be a disturbing business. There are plenty of students, let alone those who deal with students, who are upset by the turmoil and risk of it all. But Christ never promised comfort. He promised significance in the struggle and communication in relationships. He promised truth and love and freedom, now an undivided vision, and in the end a single joy.

For further reading

I know of no more than bits and pieces, but they may be suggestive. J. A. T. Robinson's *The New Reformation?* (SCM Press, London, and Westminster Press, Philadelphia), contains much that is relevant, particularly a chapter on 'a genuinely lay theology'. R. S. Peters, *Education as Initiation* (University of London Institute of Education), is a most enlightening and constructive inaugural lecture by a professor of the philosophy of education. *Student World*, No. 3, 1963, contains autobiographical accounts of Christians within various worldly situations. The interpretation of the ecumenical movement in the closing paragraphs above is set out much more fully in 'Towards a secular meaning of the ecumenical', by Albert van den Heuvel, in *Youth*, No. 10 (World Council of Churches), included in his book of essays on *The Humiliation of the Church* (SCM Press, London, and Westminster Press, Philadelphia).